From the Hood to Hollywood
A Soldier's Story

Debra J. Carroll

Copyright © 2018 by Debra Carroll

All rights reserved. No part of this publication may be reproduced or transmitted in any form or by any means, electronic or mechanical, including photocopy, recording, or any information storage and retrieval system, without permission in writing from the author.

For information about permission to reproduce selections from this book, write to facebook.com/dorchesterentertainment

Library of Congress Cataloging-in-Publication Data

ISBN-13: 978-1726196413
ISBN-10: 1726196410

Cover design by Debra Carroll
Book design by Jeani Eismont
of Eismont Design Studio

DEDICATION

This book is dedicated to my brother Donny.
May he once and for all be heard.

*"In the confrontation
between the stream and the rock,
the stream always wins – not through strength,
but by perseverance."* —H. Jackson Brown

ACKNOWLEDGEMENTS

I would like to thank the people who stood behind me and believed in my reasons for writing this book. I would also like to thank a certain attorney who took the time to listen to my story and who also believed this story was worth telling. Thanks Jeff!

Some names have been changed or omitted to their protect identity.

2015

A Soldier's Story

ABOUT THE AUTHOR

Debra J. Carroll was born and raised in Boston, Massachusetts where truth is common ground, and boldness an asset. She is an artist by nature who loves to draw. Animals will always be her first passion. Debra has a degree in Multimedia Design from Platt College, San Diego. She also studied fine art and writing at UMass Boston.

With several works in progress, Debra recently completed her first feature-length screenplay, "Fire Within." Her passion for writing developed at an early age with poetry, some of which have been published in newspapers and anthologies.

Writing for the 'big screen' is a dream of hers.

PREFACE

This book is my brother's story. I love my brother. I wrote this book because Mark Wahlberg, along with his manager Eric Weinstein and HBO appropriated my brother's original idea to "do a show about Mark's entourage." My brother Donny Carroll worked for the actor, Mark Wahlberg from the beginning of Mark's Hollywood career. He argued with Wahlberg for ten years that they should do a show about Mark's entourage, but Mark continually shot down his idea, insisting "nobody would care!" Donny knew deep down that a show about the "entourage" was a brilliant idea.

There is no question that Turtle's character was, in fact, modeled after my brother Donny, who in real life was known as "Donkey" not "Turtle." Everyone who knew him was aware that the show was his idea. There was so much controversy over it that even *60 Minutes* ran a segment a few years ago about who came up with the original idea for the show. They flat out asked Mark Wahlberg, "was the show your idea?" Mark actually stumbled over his words as he replied, "it depends on who you ask."

This book was written to set the record straight once and for all. Somewhere in HBO's files is a consent form that was signed by my brother that proves that he was, at least, the inspiration for Turtle's character and yet he was never compensated for his creative role in the hit TV show *Entourage*.

This is the way I remember how my brother's "best friend" betrayed him. Hollywood can be a dark place at times.

For me, writing this book was a quest for justice and for my brother to get the credit and recognition he legally and rightfully deserves. Without Donny's original idea, *Entourage* would never have existed, and HBO would not have cashed in on the hundreds of millions they made at his expense. What they did to my brother was wrong—plain and simple. Surely, they could have "taken care of him" as they put it, when they reassured him that he would be paid. Sometimes famous people think they have more power than the rest of us, but they are sadly mistaken.

This book has not been an easy task, nor was it something that was pleasant for me to write about. It was painful at times, infuriating at others, as I recalled the drama our family went through over this entire ordeal. Being associated with Mark Wahlberg has been a thorn in our sides. I have debated about publishing this book because I do not want to deal with any repercussions. I really just wanted to put this behind me so I can move on knowing that I did everything in my power to get this story out. I believe with all my heart this is the right thing to do.

During the course of writing this book, I had "words" with some of Mark's people. They weren't pleasant, to say the least, but I have yet to hear from Mark, despite my many attempts to reach out to him. I even sent him a copy of this manuscript! He just doesn't care about anyone but himself. Any kindness or generosity he shows is simply a disguise to cover up the selfish person he really is. How can you trust a person who stabs their most loyal and best friend in the back?

This book has taken over ten years to finish. It should have been published years ago. Due to its controversial nature, finding a publisher is not easy.

I know most people do not read the preface of a book, in fact, I wasn't sure that I would even include one. But to those who are reading this, I thank you for taking the extra five minutes to do so. I worked long and hard on this and it means a lot to me that you are reading it now. It is a very interesting story. I assure you will not be bored.

I'm not really concerned with who is offended as a result of this book.

I love playing the victim's advocate and will always fight for justice. So don't shoot the messenger! I am telling my brother's story—a story that he intended to tell. A story about friendship and loyalty. And sometimes, there is no happy ending.

Please remember not to judge me because I am telling his story. I am a justice seeker. There may be people out there who think it's wrong of me to expose this story. Mark betrayed my brother, he betrayed my family. My family was hurt. This is the way I remember it. Wahlberg is nothing to me or my family. Furthermore…nobody messes with a Carroll.

CONTENTS

1   Donny's Billion Dollar Idea 11
2   How It All Started 15
3   I Will Call Him "Marky Mark" 20
4   Rolling With The Stars 25
5   Royal Treatment 29
6   The Perpetual No 32
7   Rezawar Dawgz 34
8   Entourage 37
9   The "Donkey" Becomes The "Turtle" 40
10   Chuck Wepner 43
11   Season Two 45
12   Jason 48
13   The New Regime 52
14   Donny Goes To The Newspaper 56
15   The Official Falling Out 60
16   December 18th 66
17   Gold Diggers 71
18   Saying Goodbye 77
19   Left Behind 85
20   The Wannabe's 91
21   Time Heals 94
22   Reflections 97
23   Lightning Strikes Twice 100
24   60 Minutes 107
25   Letters to Mark 111
26   Dead End Lawyers 116

27	New York Daily New	119
28	Million Dollar Homes	122
29	Entourage; The Movie	125
30	Christmas	129
31	The Truth About Turtle	132
32	The Box Office	135

Wikipedia 136
End Notes 137
Links 138

1

Donny's Billion Dollar Idea

My brother's name was Donald Joseph Carroll. He was born in Boston, Massachusetts on December 10, 1966 to Linda and Donald Carroll. I'd like to give you some basic information about him so you have a clear understanding of who he was and what his association with Mark Wahlberg was, and how the hit television show *Entourage* came about.

If I had to squeeze his character into a nutshell, I would simply say that my brother was a good person with an enormous heart. He mastered the craft of friendship, and he was loved by everyone who knew him.

Donny, as we called him, came from a small family; it was just him, my sister, and me. He did not stray too far outside his immediate circle. I always knew he loved us very much. He was close with our parents and both of us. He probably called my mother about six times a day if not more. Yeah, I admit…he was a bit of a *mama's boy*, but it's only because he enjoyed the attention he got from her. He especially loved her cooking.

If you knew him, you could see that he had stars in his eyes. You couldn't help but noticed the way his eyes grew wide and his face lit up each time he told you one of his "get rich quick" ideas. He had always wanted to be a performer or an actor, but one thing was certain, it was Hollywood for sure!

I remember telling Donny that I would help him write some music. It wasn't until he showed me a song he had written, that I realized for the first time, how talented he really was. I wasn't too surprised, because he didn't start writing until he was older…around the time rap music took off. After hearing the sophistication in his lyrics, I remember telling him…"You don't even need my help."

My brother wanted to do something big in his life. When the opportunity presented itself to work alongside his buddy, Mark Wahlberg, he was all over that! I mean, who wouldn't be? He lived life as if every day were his last.

He never stopped talking to whomever would listen to all his clever ideas. In fact, one of the main reasons I needed to write this book was because I also understood the pain he felt, coming so close to something so big, and then having it all taken from him. He was my connection to Hollywood, too! I went to college for Multimedia Design, so Donny was my ticket to working in the entertainment industry. So, yes…I know that empty feeling of having your dreams stepped on.

Maybe that's why this story is so personal. You could say it was a chain reaction. But nothing compared to what my brother went through. I felt so heartbroken for him. Everyone knows how hard it is to make it in Hollywood. But he had the passion it takes to make it. I've studied Hollywood formula's that cover everything from scriptwriting to budgets, even books that say straight up, that "you've got to know someone" to break into the industry.

The good news is that anything is possible. Someone could be a secretary or a mailroom clerk whom you meet through a mutual friend, who happened to work for Paramount Pictures. You end up making small talk and they just might say…"I'd be happy to drop your script off on my boss's desk." And just like that you've made a connection!

Many people dream about or just talk about "going to California" or "New York". But not too many people will leave everything they know behind. Most are paralyzed by fear of the unknown.

My brother was fearless. He believed in himself, and I believed in him. He spent long periods of time away from his only child to be part of Mark's 'entourage.' It tore him up inside. He was homesick at times, but he did it because he was on a mission to make something bigger happen in his life. He wanted his daughter to have the finer things in life, and he also wanted to take care of us, his family.

He wanted so badly for our Dad to be proud of him. Donny used to promise us the world. I can still hear him saying…"I'm going to get Dad a Corvette." They talked about the color and what model they would get. Dad insisted on red even though he knew red cars got stopped by police more often. That still makes me smile.

Donny and I talked about how we'd get rich and our whole family would have a family compound like the Kennedys have on Cape Cod. I have to say, for an average city family, none of us were ever afraid to dream big. We often talked about all the dogs we would get to guard the property. "We need some German Shepherds," I'd say. Not only are they great pets, but dogs are naturally protective. Donny would put in his two cents, "I got to have some Pittie's, too." He always loved tough looking dogs and had a special fondness for Pit Bulls.

At the time I was graduating design school in San Diego, my brother was living 'the big life' 123 miles north in Los Angeles. He had serious connections in Los Angeles, and things were finally looking up! Donny had come to be somewhat of a local celebrity because of his affiliation with Mark Wahlberg. We often got VIP passes to get into clubs downtown. I remember bypassing the lines and thinking…"I could really get used to this."

Being Donny's sister, he told me a lot about his life with Mark. Some of the stuff he told me I wouldn't repeat. His adventures with Mark were at times wild, and at times mild, but there were no dull moments.

My parents got to hang out with George Clooney on the set of "The Perfect Storm." We even have a signed script from the cast, and Clooney signed a photograph for my mother, who couldn't believe that she actually got to breathe the same air as his, let alone talk to him face to face! My Dad also has coats and hats from various movie premiers that my brother attended.

On occasion, my brother, Mark, and some of the gang would drop in on my mother to indulge in her homemade Italian cooking before catching a plane back to LA or New York.

It wasn't long after he was living the big life, that Donny began to tell us about his idea for a show about Mark's entourage. He saw opportunity in everything. All he ever talked about were their adventures and how it would make such a good TV show. If Mark's fans only knew some of the things they did! I won't elaborate on anything, especially that trip to Japan.

But Donny saw this as an opportunity to do a show about himself and his life style—kind of a 'behind the scenes look' at what it's like to roll with the stars. By now, being Mark's best friend, my brother thought Mark would help him out. I remember when he called me out of frustration, when Mark blew off his ideas. But I would usually defend Mark.

"You know he's a busy person," I'd say in Mark's defense.

"He always shoots down my ideas," Donny complained.

That was pretty much the beginning of it all. Unfortunately, my brother learned firsthand about the 'cutthroat' industry of Hollywood, and how money and greed can destroy friendships and even lives. He also learned what it felt like to be knifed in the back by his 'best buddy.'

2

How It All Started

I guess you could say it all started when the Wahlbergs started hanging around Savin Hill, a tough city neighborhood of Dorchester, Massachusetts. Maybe they were always there, but we only met them when we were old enough to venture further than the security of our own street corner.

I first met Donnie Wahlberg when I was 13 years old at Savin Hill train station. There was no way I could forget a cute blonde boy who wore a red Michael Jackson coat with MJ buttons pinned in a straight line along the zipper. Not quite the normal look around our otherwise tough, multicultural neighborhood. He approached my friends and me on our way to school one day. We stood there lighting our cigarettes as we sized him up. Girls from Boston are not usually flattered by first impressions. We always have our guard up. But he was not the least bit shy. He spoke first.

"Hey, I can dance like Michael Jackson, you want to see?" He taunted. We girls exchanged glances. He was cute, so we thought we'd humor him. "I guess so," was all I managed to come up with as I took a long drag off my smoke.

And right there on the platform of Savin Hill Train station in Dorchester, he busted out with the moon walk! Truthfully, my friends thought he was a complete weirdo. We were all smiling and giggling. I kind of envied his passion and admiration of Michael Jackson. He had the kind of courage that I could only dare dream of. He wasn't afraid to dream big.

I began to see Donnie around the neighborhood more after that, but all I really knew was that his name was Donnie Wahlberg. Just a few years later, he was part of one of the most famous American boy bands at the time, and I found myself saying...

"Hey, I know that kid!"

I met his brother, Mark Wahlberg, a few years after my brother Donny met him. Just so you're not confused here, both our brothers had the same name only spelled differently. My brother spelled his with a "Y" at the end. Anyway, I started seeing Mark around more. Usually, he was riding a bike. I remembered him because, though he was 16 years old, he looked 12. Nobody could believe how young he looked. He was nice to me and my friends, and occasionally would drive us to high school in South Boston (aka Southie). Mark was just a regular boy, getting into trouble like most of us city kids who had nothing better to do.

People in the neighborhood started treating us differently because we knew the Wahlbergs. It goes to show how shallow people really are. We should have been rewarded just for having to listen to all the *New Kids'* BS alone. I'm not sure a lot of people know that Mark was an original member of *New Kids On The Block*. He just didn't fit the 'pretty boy' image of his brother, Donnie. He soon left the group and was replaced by Joey McIntyre. My brother and Mark soon got to know each other well, and over the years became inseparable.

Fast forward to the end of the whole *New Kids'* mania. Mark got his big break when his brother Donnie produced Mark's first hit "Good Vibration."

My brother Donny (aka Donkey) was, of course, by Mark's side from day one. Donny knew him when he was a regular person and got to experience what it was like to be with a big star while working for Mark's entourage for the next fourteen years. He has been places that some of us can only dream of, and certainly done more in his 39 years than some of us will ever do in a lifetime. Donny enjoyed the ride while it lasted, but he could not ignore his desire for more. He could taste the fame. Who could blame him? These very adventures are what inspired him to create a documentary about himself. He spoke candidly about his idea in a *Boston Herald* interview in June of 2005. The full article is included in a later chapter. Here is a clip:

"I told Mark I wanted to do a reality show about me," he said. "I had an idea for a book, too. It was called '*From the Hood to Hollywood – A Soldier's Story*.' It was about a kid like me who grows up with a kid like Mark and ends up in Hollywood with him, livin' the life. But Mark said, 'No one cares about that.'"

Donny knew he had a good idea and couldn't understand why Mark never gave it any serious thought. The only thing he was left to assume was that Mark was too busy, or didn't want to help his friends succeed. A close friend once told Donny in reference to Mark…"He just doesn't want his friends to blow up."

God forbid someone else from Dorchester ends up being a big star! Of course Mark didn't want that! The funny thing is he got started because his brother gave him a break. I mean who walks away from *New Kids on The Block* and actually lands in something better? But Donnie Wahlberg opened the door for Mark. I think he forgets that. He would have been nothing if it weren't for his famous brother, just like *Entourage* wouldn't have existed without my "not so famous" brother.

So, yeah, it gets annoying to have to smile at people who are oblivious to the situation. And do we dare explain? I mean, just think about what I have to go through every time I meet people. Usually the first question I get is …

"What part of New York are you from?"

Once I clarify that it's a Boston accent they are hearing, the next question is usually…"Oh my God! Do you know Mark Wahlberg?"

And my response is usually…"How much time do you have?"

OK, so not really, but you get the picture. Instead I have to bite my tongue as I listen to people rant and rave about his stupid movies. I'm not a good liar, so I usually admit I know him, but that he "cut my brother's throat" and my family is no longer on good terms with him. I mean how can I not blurt it out when it's on the tip of my tongue? I can hardly concentrate at the mere mention of Mark's name, let alone try to follow what they are saying. But you should see the look on people's faces after that. I know exactly what they are thinking. They are thinking 'what the hell did I get myself into?'

But thank God for the internet! This information about my brother is no secret, it's all over the place! *Google* his name and dozens of references will come up. Unfortunately, when you type in Donny's name, everything "Mark Wahlberg" comes up. This book is an attempt to set the records straight so that all those articles will end with: "the family of Donny Carroll went on to write a tell-all book to set the record straight."

There was a time that I used to be proud to say…"I know Mark Wahlberg. He's my brother's best friend."

You should see the looks I get when they hear that! Of course, that was long before the whole *Entourage* scandal. It's true that greed can tear people apart. Once he stabbed my brother in the back, things changed. Now the questions are more like…"Is it true your brother is Turtle?"

And my response is usually…"How much time do you have?"

People get so excited and start asking questions about the show and can't believe we don't watch it. I am sick and tired of telling a story that people don't believe anyway. Go to *Wikipedia* and type in "Turtle from *Entourage*." It clearly shows my brother was, in fact, the inspiration for Turtle's character. Even if the show wasn't his idea, they still used his character and never paid him for appropriating his life as they promised. When it comes down to it, it doesn't even matter who's idea it was—they were modeling a main character after him! Surely, he would be rich from that alone! There was no doubt a 'verbal intent to pay.' If you need more proof, go to my brother's website, www.rezawardawgz.com, and look at pictures of him and you will see Turtle's resemblance!

I certainly have better things to do than make false claims. It's just a known fact by people who knew Donny. The show was my brother's idea and everyone in the neighborhood knew it. But the "Wannabes" protect Mark. Do they actually think their loyalty will pay off? That's the biggest joke of all! The funniest part is that Mark Wahlberg and his greedy manager, Eric, actually have convinced themselves that the show really *was* their idea as you will later see.

3

I Will Call Him 'Marky Mark'

Around the time Wahlberg made his mark on the world as 'Marky Mark', my brother had become quite accustomed to shining alongside the newfound star. Marky Mark embraced hip hop, and inspired many friends when he launched his first album, *Music for the People,* followed by a later album, *You Got to Believe.* Once again, here was another white rapper and he was from our neighborhood! My brother would come home from his trips and tell me stories about how he and Marky Mark had lunch with Solieil Moon (Punkie Brewster), and how hot she was. He was definitely a charmer, a typical ladies man who told women what they wanted to hear. But love? That was another story. Donny had a way of making people laugh and every girl that dated him thought he was funny.

And then there was the story about Rachel. A famous friend of Marky Marks at the time, and how they would hang out on occasions. One particular memory stands out. Donny called me one day and he was unusually upset.

"Rachel's a fucking idiot," he said.

I started laughing, all the while encouraging him to go on.

"Why, what did she do?" I asked?

Let me state for the record that my brother was a HUGE animal lover. We both loved snakes and the iguana's, but we were definitely "dog people." So when he called me this particular day, literally crying, because Rachel had accidentally let Marky Mark's dog out, I completely understood how serious it was.

The dog got loose, ran into the street, and was consequently hit by a car. My brother stayed in the hospital with the dog, day and night, as if it were his child, and prayed for the best. Sadly, the dog lost its fight for life. My brother was completely devastated. He and Marky Mark got into a huge fight over it, and my brother ended up coming back to Boston. It was my brother, not Marky Mark who watched the dog take his last breath. Why am I not surprised? It took Donny a while to get over it. That says something about the character of the two men.

For the most part it was fun in those days. My brother would come home from long LA trips and take a bunch of us clubbing downtown where a flash of his VIP card would put us at the front of the line. He knew all the people at the restaurants and clubs. When you're seen with somebody famous often enough, people begin to recognize you and treat you like royalty. He loved flashing his newfound stardom and relished in the attention he got. Our excursions often ended in Chinatown where we'd eat until the wee hours of the morning. Donny always paid for the big meals. It made him feel important to be able to treat everyone. For him, it was the next best thing to being famous!

He was always traveling with the entourage. I don't deny that Marky Mark was good to him, but it was a job and Donny was working more often than not. In the early days, the only thing Marky Mark cared about was having his "homeboys" with him. I liked the real Marky Mark, the raw boy from Boston MUCH better than 'Mark Wahlberg, the actor.' Boy, he really does fit in with all the Hollywood cut-throats. After all he gets paid to act! I think sometimes actors have a hard time separating their careers from REALITY!

Being famous sometimes makes you wonder who your real friends are. Being best friends with a celebrity puts you in a similar situation. But back then, Marky Mark was still fresh off the street and his loyalty and friendship was not yet tainted by Hollywood greed. Back then, he was not ashamed of where he came from or to be called Marky Mark. Marky Mark once told a mutual friend in reference to Dorchester…"We got to get you out of that ghetto." But I am sure if you asked him about that, he would lie about it. His lack of loyalty to his hometown was evident when he walked out of the Super Bowl L1 because the Patriots were down. He missed the most epic comeback in Super Bowl history. It serves him right! I can't understand why people are ashamed of where they come from. I love to tell people I am from Boston and wouldn't trade my past for anything.

Being associated with Marky Mark, we enjoyed special treatment which included the best seats at concerts to back stage passes. You name it! Hollywood parties came with the territory, so my brother got to go high profile parties where Mark would warn him up front.

"No asking anyone for autographs!"

"I won't!" Donny would snap back.

People thought we were so cool because our brother got to roll with the movie stars. Hey, I wasn't complaining! Needless to say, when Donny found himself at Hollywood parties among the likes of people such as Brad Pitt or Halle Berry, he often couldn't control himself. And that is how my sister ended up with Brad Pitt's autograph and my mother ended up with George Clooney's. I never got one. But I did get my brother's! And to me, his is worth far more than theirs because he should have been a star. Sadly, he was robbed of that chance! Never the less, he was always thinking of other people and trying to find ways to make them happy. He was a bit of a show off, but in a humble way.

Donny got used to a lifestyle that some of us can only dare to dream of. He wasn't famous, but he was virtually Mark's significant other. My family often teased him about the little squabbles the two of them had. We always joked that "they were like a married couple at times." Our

I Will Call Him 'Marky Mark'

Dad would listen to Mark complain about Donny.

"All Donny wants to do is talk to girls, Mr. C," he would vent.

And yes, Donny was quite the charmer and a local hit with the girls. In the early days, he had a few girlfriends in different parts of the country. When he was home, people were always paging or calling him on the phone asking him for money and favors. Some girls would even use him in hope of getting exposure for themselves. There was one set of 'wannabe' twins, claiming to be up-and-coming models, who were always tagging along with him. I think one of them had their hand in a commercial once. At least, that's what Donny said. Anyway, one of them dated Marky Mark for a while. They never amounted to anything worth mentioning. My family could always sniff out the gold diggers. That's why we often "threw daggers" at the girls Donny brought home.

He may have been working for a famous person, but certainly wasn't making Hollywood pay in Marky's entourage. But he was paid to go everywhere Marky Mark went as long as he carried Marky's bags. There was a friendship there, but it was a job none-the-less, and after all, business is business.

My brother was right there with Marky Mark from the very beginning. He saw his friend change from being a regular person to being a star. That's something! It was even exciting to be indirectly involved. What my brother was being paid was barely enough to get by on, but it came with all-expense paid trips around the world. So who complained?

Things could only get better with more connections that my brother made. Maybe his dreams would come true after all. My family had high hopes for him. We believed in him. But he didn't want to spend his life in someone else's shadow. He knew he was fortunate to be in this situation, but he thirsted for more. He was a character indeed, and certainly had what it took to make it in Hollywood. When you see an opportunity you should go for it. Everyone he met loved him and commented on how funny he was. He wanted fame and fortune so much, he could taste it.

He was away so often that my family would give him a hard time, reminding him that he was a father now, and he should get his priorities straight. Of course, we wanted him to be part of Marky Mark's entourage, but it was a trade-off. He struggled to find balance between his family and a career. Everything he did was for the good of his family. He never stopped reaching for the stars. He loved us all very much. He had that "just wait, I'll show you" attitude.

One thing more about Marky Mark. There has been debate over who was the more successful rap artist—Marky Mark or Eminem? That was a HUGE insult to Eminem to even compare the two rappers. I mean really! Who would even suggest such nonsense? Marky who?

4

Rolling With The Stars

Being famous opens many doors. *Marky Mark and the Funky Bunch* were a hit. And even a bigger hit because Mark was the brother of the ultra-famous Donnie Wahlberg, of *New Kids On The Block*. I had one friend who used to ask to touch my shirt because I knew Donnie Wahlberg! For real! I used to laugh and say "go ahead and get your jollies!" I would tease her for being a *New Kids* groupie. I always wondered what Donnie would have thought if he knew of this residual effect he had on people.

Marky Mark was doing really well. He had a few albums under his belt and was grabbing the attention of everyone. Suddenly, America had a new bad boy, and he was from Boston! And my brother was right there in the spotlight every step of the way! In the early days of Marky Mark, Donny even got to participate on stage when Mark performed on the Arsenio Hall show.

Donny began writing his own rap songs and experimenting with music. He later teamed up with a like-minded friend, Nik-Platinum who would become his partner in crime.

Anyone who travels a lot becomes quite accustomed to living this 'double life'. But for Donny, the double life had a whole new meaning. One day he'd be breaking bread with millionaires, and the next day he'd be back on the street corner staring at melted gum on the sidewalk. I can only imagine the memories must have inevitably come crashing back into his brain. It's a harsh and bitter transition.

I'm sure rolling with the stars was great, but Donny had higher aspirations. He continued to work for Mark, but turned his focus toward making his own music when time allowed. He and Nik formed a group called *Rezawar Dawgz* and began recording songs under the name Murda One. He bragged about the fact that he had personally asked Quentin Tarantino (*Reservoir Dogs*) if he could use that name.

Donny was so funny at times when he spoke of his dreams of living large. He bragged a lot, but we knew he had to keep up appearances. He tried very hard to get his music career off the ground. There were times I felt so bad for him because I knew firsthand what it was like to desperately try to do something big and the discouragement that came with each failed attempt.

My brother enjoyed his times with Mark, but there was a lot that went on behind closed doors that people didn't know about, such as all the empty promises. Donny told Mark he wanted to do a documentary or a book about his own life. But with money comes greed. At the time, I never felt this was the case with Mark and my brother. I believed Mark shot down his ideas, year after year, simply because he was just too busy and had no time for other projects. I understood that, and told my brother that was likely the reason.

I had also dreamed of moving to Los Angeles. I studied film, special effects, 3D modeling – the whole nine yards! I graduated from college in California with a degree in Multimedia Design. I wanted to work for Universal Studios or Paramount Pictures! Better yet, my brother was going to be famous, and I would work for him! That was my dream. Instead, I couldn't find a job that paid more than $12.00 an hour in my field. I ended up doing design work on the side and then became a debt collector. The money was good if you weren't afraid to ask people for what they owed.

As a creative person I sometimes had to stifle my dreams. I know the dread of waking up every day and going to a 'regular job.' Ugh! I could count the times I have heard "you'll grow with the company," or "you'll be a manager someday." I have helped new companies get off the ground more than once, and even burned bridges on the promise of something greater. Sad to say, you might expect this from a corporation, but not from your best friend.

By now, Mark was appearing across America in ads sporting Calvin Klein underwear. Then some acting opportunities started falling in his lap. Still, my brother was beside him every step of the way. Donny saw Mark at his best and his worst moments. They were close, no doubt about that. Mark was grateful to have my brother as a friend. He knew my brother was loyal and could be trusted. Donny considered Mark "the brother he never had," and often used those exact words in describing their relationship.

Donny used to get so mad when Mark wouldn't do what he wanted, and I would have to bring him back to reality reminding him how lucky he was, and that Mark was just busy as hell.

"It's a great idea! But he's an actor, he's busy! I'm sure he's got a lot going on," I'd say.

"Everyone thinks it's a good idea! Mark can fuck off, how about that?" he'd shout.

"Donny! Listen to me! DON'T burn that bridge!" I'd rationalize.

I would calm him down and try to get him to understand. We're a stubborn family—all of us, so that's not an easy thing to do.

Mark was busy. It was as simple as that. Everyone wanted a piece of him. I'm sure his head was spinning with his new-found fame and requests from friends and family to do this or that. It was so drastically different from the life he was used to.

Even if Mark never made the show, I would have understood why. You can only do so much with the time you have. My brother got to attend elaborate events and meet lots of famous people. One of his favorite pictures was of him and Halle Berry that can be seen on his website under gallery. He traveled all over the world. Mark wined and dined him along the way. Donny knew he had it good, but it bugged him that Mark didn't share his vision for a show about the entourage.

I admired the way my brother believed in himself. It's a hard thing to do sometimes. We all play it off like we do, but deep down we have our personal doubts. With Donny, you never saw the doubt in his eyes or his heart. He knew he had what it takes and wasn't afraid to take chances. He KNEW the show was meant to be. He was already living large, just on someone else's dime; and, quite frankly, that wasn't his cup of tea. What everyone else saw as…"You're so lucky," he saw as…"I'm done being Mark's bitch."

And honestly, unless you've walked in someone else's shoes, you have no right to judge them. How would you feel if this happened to you? Imagine your best buddy steals your idea and makes billions! Try wrapping your head around that, if you dare.

I saw Donny go through many emotional ups and downs. People think the Hollywood life is all glitz and glammer, but there's a dark side that people can only learn firsthand. Donny was somewhat of a local celebrity, and not solely by his affiliation with Wahlberg. Along with this stardom, came people who begged, borrowed, and definitely stole from him. Most people certainly never paid him back. But he had a good heart and often lent a helping hand to those who harassed him enough. Then he'd spend even more money on jewelry for whomever his latest gold digger was. But that'll be another chapter in this book.

5

Royal Treatment

Who wouldn't love getting the royal treatment? Donny was used to walking into any public establishment with or without Mark and having people treat him like a god. People really liked him and enjoyed being in his company. Once you get a taste of this life, there's no turning back. My brother continued to attend parties and movie premieres while often working on the set of one of Mark's films. He seemed to enjoy the after-parties much more since that was the only time he could really relax and not have to wait on Mark hand-and-foot. Being Mark's personal assistant, the job doesn't end until you know "all's well that ends well." Donny looked out for Mark and always had his back.

When Donny was in Boston, people flocked to him like sheep to a shepherd. People clung to him trying to weasel a seat beside him on one of his many flights to L.A.

"Come on Donkey, take me, take me," his friends would beg.

I had a chance to attend one of Mark's premiere's once in Boston, but I chose not to attend. I remember my sister telling me she felt bad when they first arrived and had to wait outside.

"What are we waiting for?" she asked.

"We're just waiting for them to kick some people out," Mark said.

"Kick some people out?" she asked.

"Yeah, to make room for us," he told her.

Although she felt mighty special, she couldn't help but remember the people that got bumped just so they could have seats. Mark planned on spending a lot of money that night which is why the people got bumped to begin with. It's not just "who you are," but "how big is your bank account."

Donny would light up when telling us stories of all the places he had been with Mark. We used to tell him how lucky he was to be able to go on trips with all expenses paid. He resented our implications claiming that although there were some good times, he was "sick of carrying Mark's bags." At this point it seemed kind of beneath him, but he did it anyway hoping that his many years of loyalty might pay off someday.

Donny began focusing even more time making music, since he was certainly not getting rich working for Wahlberg. The last thing Mark would have wanted was for someone else from his neighborhood to become famous and possible outshine him. If only given the chance, Donny would have outshined him BY FAR! My brother actually had talent! Mark had a famous brother, a "baby face," and some luck to get him started. That's a monumental difference.

So, Donny still worked for Mark, but the two continued to disagree and argue about everything. The usual argument was always about doing a TV show about the entourage.

"Why can't you just pitch the idea?"

"Because nobody gives a shit!" Mark yelled.

Donny was even more determined than ever to make it on his own. He knew he couldn't depend on anyone else to help him, especially Mark. Sure, he enjoyed the fancy dinners and trips around the world, but inside, he knew he wasn't meant to ride someone else's coattails. He had good ideas, stayed true to his music, and became dedicated to writing more. Most people would have been content with just being Mark's assistant. But Donny wasn't afraid to dream big. Believing in yourself can make all the difference in the world. At the time, he didn't realize that working for Mark was keeping him just where Mark wanted him—at the bottom.

Donny told us about meeting Hollywood execs and how everyone always commented on how funny he was. Who could have known that one day HBO would feel so strongly about my brother's character that they would model a character in a hit TV show after him!

He would come back to Boston after living like a movie star for weeks at a time, and make the usual appearances on all the local street corners. He spent time reconnecting with people he knew and telling of his adventures. When the stories ran out he didn't know what else to say.

It was a very long time before my brother actually became bitter toward Mark. Everyone who knew my brother, locally, as well as their "mutual acquaintances" some of whom I've referred to as "the wannabe's," knew that the idea to do a TV show about the entourage was my brother's original idea.

6

The Perpetual No

The irony of the whole story is that for years Donny *did* bug Mark a lot about doing a show about the entourage and Mark always shot it down. Instead, Mark offered to help my brother film a documentary series about Donny's life, and even shot some film. Donny never had a chance to get the files from Mark. Indirectly, these files are some of the earliest influences for *Entourage*, since it was meant to be about Donny and his life working for Mark. He figured if Mark won't do a show, a documentary is the next best thing to having a show based on his own life and adventures with the entourage.

Once he started working on the documentary, Mark stepped in and tried playing the nice guy. This way Mark could maintain control over the situation. In the back of Mark's mind things were brewing. He was starting to think that maybe his friend was really on to something.

The documentary would not only be about Donny's association with the famous entourage, but would also feature his life as a rapper for *Rezawar Dawgz*. But the work they did together never came to anything. It was the "Perpetual No." Donny couldn't stand being told no, especially when he knew he was right.

Nothing stopped my brother. He still hounded Mark about doing the show. Many of Donny's friends and Mark's close mutual acquaintance's knew about Donny's idea. He had talked about it for ten years! But we always chalked it up as another good idea that lacked funding. One of those acquaintances had the audacity to ask me shortly after my brother's death, "You're not going to start trouble with Mark are you?"

I was dumbfounded! Me? How was I starting trouble? First of all, I want to get one thing straight. I don't start trouble…but I can certainly finish it. So, when this jerk said this to me (you know who you are), I actually thought twice about that. Was I starting trouble? Why should this be kept a secret? My brother was someone, and he wasn't here to fight for himself. The saddest thing was that this mutual friend was closer to us than to Mark, or so I thought. We had known him all our lives. But as long as my blood is flowing, I can, at least, do everything in my power to make sure people know the truth. Why should I feel bad about seeking justice for my brother? These people live in a damn fantasy world and it's about time someone slaps them back into reality. Let there, at least, always be the question in people's minds.

Initially, even my own family was divided about confronting Mark after my brother's death. We always hoped Mark would contact my parents one day, or come by and talk to them. I really thought he loved my brother. But after my brother died, we never heard from him again. We thought it was because he didn't know if we would greet him with open arms, or if one of us was going to punch him in the face.

7

Rezawar Dawgz

Donny (aka Murda One) and Nik (aka Nik Platinum) continued to work on building their first album. In the early days, it seemed like completing the album was so far out of reach. Anyone who works on something big knows what this feels like.

Rezawar Dawgz had picked out their name and were certainly on their way. They also had the one thing that most start-up groups didn't have—a famous friend named Mark Wahlberg. We were all very surprised when Wahlberg agreed to do a track with them. This was huge break for Murda and Plat. Since they were just starting out, they hadn't really focused too much on the promotional aspect. My husband began putting the website together, while I worked on logos and a look for the cover. Once Mark did the track, we could get the *Rezawar* name out there.

Mark did the track with them, but he never allowed it to be released for some reason, and we were never able to get our hands on the actual file. If it had been released, no doubt it would have jump started their music career. If I remember correctly, Mark's reason was that being an actor now, he did not want to feel like he was going backwards.

As with the documentary, Mark never saw this project through either. So, when Mark pulled some strings and got them a gig opening for the pop group, *N'Sync*, we were again surprised. We thought this could be a chance for them to really be seen. Creatively, Donny was tired of being at Mark's mercy. He didn't want to beg Mark to do a TV show that he clearly had no interest in doing. But he would take what he could get and *N'Sync* was at least a step in the right direction.

Rezawar Dawgz did open for *N'Sync*, but the arena wasn't full when they performed. I guess we never thought of it until afterward, but with concerts, most people don't show up until the main act. Donny was disappointed at the small audience, yet still happy that, at least, there was an audience, and that he could actually say the words "we opened for *N'Sync*."

Donny continued to work for Mark, but his assignments were becoming few and far between. He spent the majority of his time in Boston. He struggled to remain optimistic, and at times, doubt would creep in and disappointment would take over. He had some music under his belt now and was serious about working on building the album. *Rezawar Dawgz* had some recognition now, and despite their ups and downs, their philosophy was "never give up."

When Donny did talk to Mark about his desire to act and do a show, Mark would tell him…"Stick to rapping, you're a rapper!" Those who knew Donny, knew he was passionate about doing the show and more passionate about being in it! He wanted the full package, who wouldn't?

If Mark had taken his own advice, you'd be saying, Mark who?

He would use encouragement to brainwash Donny by convincing him to "stick to rapping." But the truth was Mark was afraid Donny would get famous either way. He never liked Donny mingling with Hollywood exec's at events. He was always telling Donny not to talk to people. Those who were closer to Donny could see the jealousy in Mark's eyes, and some even admitted that. Mark would never want anyone he knew to have a shot at fame, if he could help it. So the whole attempt to do a track was just a scheme to hold Donny back and get his mind off doing a show.

8

Entourage

As time went on, Donny grew tired of marks lies and broken promises. He was grateful for the *N'Sync* gig, but it really did nothing for *Rezawar Dawgz*. He worked on his music, but remained distant from Mark. He still loved and cared about him, but he finally realized that no matter how hard he tried to get Mark to help him get exposure, Mark never saw anything through. And then one day, months later, I received a call from my brother.

"You're never going to believe it," he said.

"What?" I asked as my anticipation grew.

"Mark pitched my idea to HBO, they want to do the show!"

"Oh my God! What? Are you serious?" I shouted back?

I could feel the look of shock on my face. It felt like we hit the lottery! He'd been talking about this for ten years! My mind began to race. I couldn't even think straight! His voice brought me back.

"Can you believe it? They want to do a show about the entourage! See? I fucking told Mark all along!"

He couldn't believe it either. Most things that seem too good to be true usually are. It's good to go through life with big dreams, but when it actually knocks on your door, you still don't believe it. My brother was going to be rich! I was so happy for him, and naturally, for what this meant for our family. This meant we could all be together. This meant the family compound we'd all dreamed about would come true! I knew it! I knew this day would come! "So this is what it feels like," is what I was thinking.

Life would have been so boring without dreams. I'd probably never have to work again! That way I could write all the books and screenplays I wanted! My brother was generous. He told us all the things he would do if he ever made it big. We were all like that. My dad played the lottery faithfully; my husband and I had started our own design business with the hope of building an elite clientele. We even have a few celebrity clients that were referred to us from Donny. My brother had waited so long for this. We really thought this was it! That was the moment our world would be forever changed. Only not the way we had hoped for.

Donny was so excited. He told everyone about it, still saying that he couldn't believe Mark finally took him seriously. After all the years of talking about doing an entourage show, *Entourage* was actually in the works! Donny was even going to audition for a part! He was beside himself. He was much more excited at the chance to be an actor than for the show itself. He would read for the character they would call "Turtle," who would be modeled after his own life with Mark. Excitement was everywhere.

A team of people studied him from head-to-toe in an attempt to ensure accuracy when recreating the fictional character. Of course, with all this came a consent form. So Wahlberg had him sign a release that read, in part:

As you are aware, there is a character in the program presently named 'Turtle.' Although the character is intended to depict a fictional person, the name is similar to your nickname and the character may exhibit certain characteristics that are similar to yours or be involved in certain events that are similar to events that you may be involved in.

Donny signed the form. I remember scolding him for signing anything without telling us. My sister worked with one of Boston's most prestigious law firms at the time, and could easily have had the document reviewed so that he would have known what he was signing. He was insulted that I implied that they would trick him.

"What do you think I'm stupid?" he yelled.

"Never, ever, ever sign anything without knowing what you're signing!" I replied.

He told me that Mark and Eric reassured him time and time again that "he would be taken care of." Donny believed them, of course. Why would he have any reason not to? This was his best friend for nearly fourteen years! Good friends are generally loyal where we come from. I never in a million years would have believed Mark would screw Donny over if I hadn't seen it with my own two eyes.

9

The "Donkey" Becomes The "Turtle"

On the day of the audition, Donny was a natural. The HBO executives loved him. After all, they knew enough about him to want to model a character after him. Donny was elated. He was one step closer to that moment he had waited so very long for—that moment when he crossed that proverbial line between two drastically different worlds. When the news came later that the writers had decided to cast younger, New York natives, Donny was blown away.

"It's not the end of the world," I said.

"I wanted to play myself!" he cried.

"You're still getting rich, so who cares?" I told him.

"Mark said they want to go with younger actors in case the show's a hit," he added.

In my mind, I could see the way his eyebrows would come together as he pouted like a little boy who's just dropped his ice cream cone. Disappointing as it was, it did make sense that they would use younger people, a smart decision…a business decision. He would get rich anyway, so it didn't even matter. It was, after all, his concept to begin with.

So I said, "I think that's smart thinking."

And that's what we were led to believe, that they had simply decided to use younger actors. HBO still modeled a main character after him, so he was set to cash in either way. Mark led him to believe that it didn't matter who played "Turtle"—the "Donkey" would be paid.

But Donny wanted fame. I knew how badly he wanted to be a big Hollywood actor. And it doesn't come much closer than this! This was his one chance to really shoot for the stars!

Famous people forget what it's like to be able to walk down the street without being ambushed by a mob, which likely includes a handful of crazies. What kind of life can that really be? Acting is not all it is cracked up to be. I bet most actors wish they could keep their money and lose the mob scenes. But the fans are the ones who put them where they are, and it comes with the territory. I don't envy that at all! I'd rather work "behind the scenes" when working in the industry, but if someone offered me ten million to hear my authentic Boston accent in the next Ben Affleck movie, I'd be all over that. Any takers?

It's ridiculous that people obsess over celebrities. My mother could never understand why I didn't want to listen to her stories about "Britney" and "Celine." She would talk about them like they were friends of hers. She'd go on and on about "Britney" and I'd say, "Britney who?"

"Spears!" she'd scream, nearly taking my head off.

Even film instructors preach that actors get the most credit and they deserve the least. Acting is an art, but the person who's concept it was, the person who's original idea it was, the one who takes the time to execute a screenplay or a book—*they* are the ones who deserve the most credit! Donny is the one who deserves the credit that this whole book is based upon.

In the "industry," let's not forget it is a business. Salaries are inflated approximately five times. But the one who gets the most credit for the all the movies is always the "the actor." Every movie producer will tell you one thing, and that is, "concept is king."

You may hear someone say, "Did you see that Mark Wahlberg movie?" When they should be saying, "Did you see that Sebastian Junger movie?" You never heard of Sebastian Junger? Oh, that's because the people who wrote the story get the least amount of credit. Sebastian Junger wrote *The Perfect Storm*, but probably all you remember is George Clooney and Mark Wahlberg, right?

So the people with the ideas never seem to get the money, but they can cash in and sell their ideas. You can't have anything without first having a good idea, right? And the reality is that great ideas are stolen every day. Or you can just give your idea away, seemingly like my brother did. Sounds ridiculous that someone who spent their life trying to get rich would give away a billion dollar idea just like that…unless he was told he'd be taken care of by people he knew for a long time and trusted wholeheartedly. So instead of Donny Carroll getting famous playing "Turtle," a character that was modeled after his very person, Jerry Ferrara got rich and famous instead by portraying in essence…" Donny Carroll."

Without my brother's original idea, nothing *ENTOURAGE* would exist. That includes syndicated box sets in all countries, T-shirts, lunch boxes, and all the garbage that people make money from.

10

Chuck Wepner

Chuck Wepner, nicknamed "the bayonne bleeder," was a professional boxer in the '60s from Bayonne, New Jersey. He had boxed while serving in the United States Marine Corp and worked several jobs as a bouncer before becoming a professional boxer. During Wepner's career, he lost quite a few fights. He was not expected to make a name for himself until a string of losses turned into a string of wins. Wepner, indeed, made a name for himself, winning nine of his next eleven fights which included victories against former Heavy Weight Champions.

In 1975 Wepner challenged Muhammad Ali for the World's Heavyweight title. According to an article in *Time Magazine,* "In Stiches," Ali was guaranteed a sum of $1.5 million while Wepner was only guaranteed $100k. For Wepner, this was a large enough sum of money that he accepted the contract readily.

Wepner, along with his manager, Al Braverman and trainer, Bill Prezant, spent eight weeks near the Catskill Mountains training for the big event which was held on March 24, 1975 at the Richfield Coliseum in Ohio. On the big day, Wepner knocked Ali down in the ninth round and thought he had defeated the champ. An angry Ali got up, and the fight continued. Ali knocked Wepner down with nineteen seconds left in the 15th round. The referee counted to seven before he called it a technical knockout.

Wepner then fought professional wrestler, Andre the Giant in 1976 and lost. It has long been rumored that Sylvester Stallone watched Wepner's fight on his home TV and was inspired to write the script for *Rocky*. It has also been speculated that this was where Stallone's inspiration for *Rocky III* came from. Although Stallone denies these claims, it was no secret in Wepner's home town knew who the real "Rocky" was.

Throughout the *Rocky* era, Wepner met and became friendly with Stallone, and it was no secret that he was the inspiration for the films. Although he enjoyed all the attention that came with being "the real Rocky," he was never paid a penny by Stallone for using his stories. If you listen to Wepner's interview on *Youtube* (Chuck Wepner), he recounts claims of how Stallone would visit him from time to time. Wepner met other famous people as a result of his connection to Stallone. He was even photographed with Robert Dinero.

Wepner was later sent to jail for irrelevant reasons. While imprisoned, Stallone again visited him playing "good guy," asking Wepner "is there anything you need?" Shortly after that visit, Stallone filmed a movie in Wepner's hometown called "Bad Money," which included scenes that were once again, very similar to events in Wepner's life. This time, however, Stallone never even had the courtesy to let Wepner know he was filming locally, not to mention that the movie was a rip-off of Wepner's life. By now, Wepner had enough. He ultimately hired a lawyer and sued Stallone. Wepner won the lawsuit and settled with Stallone for an undisclosed amount of money.

It should be obvious why I told you the story of Chuck Wepner and Sylvester Stallone. People are just greedy. It's a shame that money is more important than loyalty, love, and respect. I admire Chuck for fighting for justice.

11

Season Two

*E*ntourage was a huge success. By now our family realized that Donny was definitely being screwed over. The show was about to kick off their second season and was doing great. Mark continued to feed Donny bullshit to buy himself more time. It was clearly a stall tactic. In any case, my brother, who spent more than a decade of his life being loyal to his "best friend," began to see things in a new light. The bitterness began to eat him alive. There was no reason why he should not be getting some compensation from the show.

Mark's crooked manager, Eric Weinstein, is more of a liar than Mark. According to Donny, even Eric reassured him that he would be paid and not to worry about anything, even though season one had passed without a cent! And the worst part…the most insulting part, was that Eric got a producer's credit and Donny never got any credit! Talk about a knife in the back! This rumor is widely publicized online and only supports my claim.

My brother was by Mark's side from day one and could have sold him out on many occasions for a quick buck, but he never did. Mark knew the show was Donny's idea, but over the years has really tried to convince himself that the show was his own original idea.

I told my brother time and again, "don't burn that bridge!" But in the end, even I realized that Mark really had screwed him over. How else can I put it? After years of telling Donny not to burn that bridge, I finally had to admit, "I think, at this point, it is safe to assume you're being screwed over."

I had truly believed Mark would come through. My whole family did. We were all very surprised and disappointed in him. To this day, we have questions as to why, or how, he could have done such a horrible thing to his best friend. He actually gets on TV and has the audacity to refer to my brother that way. My parents have a copy from an old Regis show where he refers to Donny as "his best friend."

We used to believe Mark really cared, however I can only assume by his lack of compassion, that he only cares about himself. Mark's colorful past is posted all over the internet. I used to cut Mark some slack since we grew up in the same neighborhood. I'm sure we've all done things we're not proud of. I know I have! I thought he was a genuinely good person, but when you look at the kind of things he has done, compared to my brother who never harmed ANYONE in his whole life, who are you going to believe?

Even if the show was not his idea (although everyone knows it was), the Turtle character is still based on Donny and HBO has proof of this! They must have really thought he was a fool. And some of you may think, "shame on him for not registering his ideas"...but remember, we're talking about his BEST FRIEND of fourteen years with whom he was collaborating. Donny had no idea he was being robbed of his intellectual property. HBO flat out told him that he'd be "taken care of." What else does that mean? They sure took care of him alright! They took him all the way to the cleaners!

Around this time, my brother completely started to blow Mark off. He still ranted and raved to anyone who would listen. Mark still tried to act like his friend, knowing damn well what he had done. Did he really think Donny would just sit there and let HBO steal his character, let alone HIS show? They must have, because that's exactly what they did.

My brother became very quiet and withdrawn. He was trying to deal with the pain of being knifed in the back by his long time buddy after being led to believe he was going to be rich. That's a tough pill to swallow for anyone. Donny was beginning to realize his dreams were not manifesting quite the way he had imagined. We began to see a side of Donny that we had never seen before.

He tried to listen to the advice of real friends who would tell him to forget about Mark and just do his own thing. Donny had pride. He tried hard to pull it together, but you could just see that he was broken inside. That sense of humor that defined him was slowly replaced by despair. The wannabes tried to minimize my brother's feelings by staying loyal to Mark, as if it would somehow pay off. Who has a right to judge how he felt? That's the biggest joke of all. They are all a bunch of fools. Everyone knows Mark is a cutthroat.

As the distance grew between Mark and Donny, stories began to emerge online referencing the falling out that the two of them had with regard to the show. Media sources began contacting Donny, soliciting him for "his side of the story." But he always had hope that Mark would eventually come through as he had promised.

In a court of law any smart person would know that someone, who is desperate to be rich, wouldn't sign away his rights to a television show. Eric Weinstein coerced my brother into signing a consent form by leading him to believe he was signing a form that merely gave HBO permission to model a character after him. This is what they told him. You know, just a formality. He believed that this was what was needed in order for the production to move forward.

If you have ideas or are trying to get into the entertainment industry, make sure you register your ideas and your scripts with associated guilds. Document and copyright your original work. Even the poor man's copyright still works which is when you mail yourself the document and leave it sealed. Even computer files retain dates and can prove the original date of a document. I guess it's a lesson to be learned.

12

Jason

Jason was a good friend of ours. To know what kind of person he was, I'll tell you a little story. One night I came home very late. A friend dropped me off near my house. I got out of the car and my friend drove away. The night was silent except for the crickets you hear on summer nights. I began walking toward my house, when suddenly, I heard…"Pssssst."

It was past midnight, but as I strained to see where the voice had come from, I was able to make out the vague figures of Donny and Jason. They stood a few houses away from ours, across the street from each other, each clenching tightly to a baseball bat. Donny put his finger up to his lips.

"Shhhhhhhh," I heard him say.

"Donny?" I called out.

Just then, he and Jason emerged from the shadows and met me in the middle of the street. I looked at them peculiarly.

"What the hell are you two doing? It's after midnight!" I asked as I wondered why they had baseball bats.

"Waiting for your boyfriend," Jason replied as he swung his bat back and forth. There was a crazy man who was stalking me.

The odd part about this stalker was that I had never even met him! He was the boyfriend of a friend of a friend whom I may have seen in passing once or twice. He was a creep. But Jason and Donny had my back. That's how it was in my neighborhood. Jason would have taken a bat to someone for me because I was Donny's sister. They were more like brothers than friends.

Later, when Jason died suddenly, Donny was completely devastated. We all were. Jason was just 32 years old at the time. He was one of a kind. He was also a mutual friend of Mark's, but Jason's loyalty was with Donny. I couldn't say enough about him to give you an idea of what a great person he was. He was a wonderful friend; he was also my niece's second cousin which technically made him family.

I shared an apartment with Donny and Jason years earlier when my niece was a just a baby. Jason had a sense of humor and could make any one laugh. Did I mention how handsome he was? I'll never forget his unique, raspy voice; it was his signature trademark.

I was at work when Donny called me. His tone was melancholy. He came right out with it.

"Jason died," he said.

"What? What do you mean?" I said in disbelief.

I could tell Donny was in shock, as the words spilled out, that he just couldn't believe it! Instantly, I thought of Jason's significant other who had grown up in our neighborhood. I asked him if she knew. Our families were very close when we were young. We always thought of her like a little sister.

Donny wasn't sure if she knew. Later she told me that she got to see him and was there in his final moments, and for that she is grateful.

I was shocked. It's such a surreal feeling when you hear that someone you loved had died. I couldn't help thinking…"Another lost friend."

Unfortunately, we've lost so many friends in our young lives that you get used to that familiar shock.

Sometimes people tell me…"I had one friend who died."

And I'm thinking…"A friend?" I have lost ten or more friends from my old neighborhood in just an eight block radius! But when someone you know dies, life becomes terrifying for a while. If you've ever lost someone you love, friend or family, you know exactly what I mean. Living in the city you have to be in survival mode at all times. Every time we lose someone else, we're all thinking the same thing, which nobody dares say out loud..."Who's next?"

Jason's death hit Donny hard. He seemed to shut out the rest of the world for a while. He was so hurt over the loss that he didn't want to do anything. He stopped everything and grieved.

As ridiculous as it may sound, people have asked me throughout the years..."Is Boston really like the movie Goodwill Hunting?"

And by that they mean..."Would your friend really take a baseball bat to someone's head for you?"

My response is usually, "Just go ask some of my old friends."

I've had my share of occasions that involved baseball bats. From smashing in the hood of a car full of perverts to chasing ex-lunatics down Dorchester avenue; I've swung a baseball bat for everything except a baseball game, and I'm female! Imagine how the boys had it? The bottom line was that you had to be tough or get beat up. I didn't like it, but we had no choice. It didn't matter if you were male, female, black or white, or anything in between! We did what we had to do. And I'm glad they ask because it was a realistic portrayal of the Boston I once knew. My dad always told me, "Don't let anyone push you around."

I couldn't live with that feeling of humiliation. I would not allow myself to be a coward. A close female friend of mine and I once told her husband when he said..."Boy, you two sure know how to get in trouble." We agreed at that moment that "we would die for the cause if we had to." The only problem was, that I am not really sure what the cause was. When someone looked at me the wrong way, that was cause enough for attack. So I threw myself into trouble head first by rationalizing "they're not going to kill me!" I mean, what's the worst that could happen?

Donny had a hard time picking himself up after Jason was gone. But it would be Jason's spirit that would inspire him to stop feeling sorry for himself and make something positive happen. Many times we talked about Jason, and how he would want Donny to be happy. Inspired to do what he knew would make Jason happy, Donny jumped back into his music full force. With the help of his rap partner and friend Platinum, Donny found a new determination to go after his dreams once again.

13

The New Regime

After a lot of hard work, Murda One and Nik Plat had nearly completed their first album, "The New Regime." The album featured a handful of songs that outlined the deception of Mark Wahlberg and the whole *Entourage* scandal. The following information was actually written by the group themselves. I have only made small changes to reflect the passage of time.

Upon completion of the album, The Rezawar Dawgz launched their website in the summer of 2005. One of the songs, track #7 is titled "Every time I Close My Eyes," is about how Mark lied about everything with regard to *Entourage*. The following profiles are taken from the website as each member of the group introduced themselves.

Rezawar Dawgz was a collaboration of talent, skill and originality. The core goal of this group was to enhance the hub of innovative Hip Hop, as well as reach various fans.

This clique was not only a bunch of entertainers, but artists with attitude, heart, vision, and marketability. Rezawar Dawgz promised to bring something new to the rap game. Their influence came in part from the movie "Reservoir Dogs," and had some type of influence, including the fact that all the artists are Caucasian.

Second of all, they model themselves after the slang idea of vicious dogs. Vicious meaning hungry, no-holds bar, and ready for any type of "dog" fight (any type of battle). Their style was a concoction of straight-up Bronx and quirky Boston Hip Hop. This mixture can be related to all people that appreciate lyrics, truth, and great beats.

PROFILES

*Nik Platinum's popular quote: "My name is Nik and the name Platinum comes from the idea that I am a rare and unique element." Born and raised in the Bronx where Hip Hop originated and was created. He has always inspired to be the first "Albanian and white" artist directly from the Bronx. His role models were, and always will be, Run DMC, LL Cool J, Eric B. and Rakim, and the Beastie Boys. Back in the '80s, he was one of the first break-dancers with the cardboard dance floor and everything. Just for fun, he earned his ranks in the streets rhyming with no beats to help his flow take off. He became known as the only white boy that could really rhyme. His countless shows in the underground rap industry have brought about confidence and resilient entertaining abilities. Later in his life he met up with people such as Mark Wahlberg and established a friendship, which eventually led to his companionship with Donny C, a.k.a Murda One.

*Murda One: Donny grew up in Dorchester, one of the toughest neighborhoods in Boston. Hanging out with the wrong crowd, he hustled to make ends meet to provide for his daughter. With the sudden celebrity status of his childhood friend, Mark Wahlberg, Donny embarked on a long journey traveling with him to various parts of the world living a life he had never imagined possible. That was his first real taste of the rich life and that experience has driven him to emulate that lifestyle for himself. For over a decade, he has proved his devotion to Mark from being a soldier in the days of "Marky Mark's" group to being his personal assistant. However, since meeting with Nik Platinum his underlying passion for rapping has resurfaced and intensified. His style is unique due to the Boston accent, which will leave fans wanting more. HBO's hit original series *Entourage* has based the character "Turtle" on Murda One.

*Mario C: The overly talented producer and DJ of the Rezawar Dawgz, has created beats that are matchless and original. His perfectionism has brought about beats that tunes into all the senses. Being raised in the Bronx with experience in the DJ business has proven no competition for him to this day. Mario also was into graffiti (Tags) and breakdancing.

The Dawgz were up and coming and even went on to release a video of their popular track "4 Da Streets" which contains footage of Mark Wahlberg as he introduces Murda and Plat.

Donny made us cut Mark out of the video. One day he called me up really pissed off.

"Fuck Mark, take him out, I don't need him," he complained.

"Just leave him in there!" I argued back.

"I don't need him to make it," he pleaded.

And it's true that Donny was now more determined than ever to prove that he was somebody and that he didn't need Mark Wahlberg's name to make him famous. After all, he'd just spent years trying to get Mark to do a show about them, and that still didn't make him famous.

It was a major turning point for Donny to accept that Mark had actually "cut his throat." He was far more hurt than angry. But he had to go through the hurt and the anger in order to move forward. Holding on to pain and anger is not good for anyone. The reason for this book is so that my family can know in our hearts, that we tried everything possible to get the credit and recognition Donny deserved for his creative part in *Entourage*. We are looking forward to putting this behind us.

So we removed Mark from the video. Then a week later, Donny called me back.

"Fuck him, put him back," he said.

We weren't too happy about having to spend more hours putting Mark back in the video, but we chuckled at Donny's childish temper at times. I agreed with him that it was best to leave Wahlberg in, and by now Mark damn well owed Donny big time! May as well take what you can get from the jerk! So, needless to say, he is in the video which can also be seen on www.rezawardawgz.com and clicking on video release.

The video was dedicated to Jason's memory. A while after Jason died,

Donny's outlook on life changed a little. He knew by finishing his album and video that Jason would be proud of him. Jason always told him to focus on his own thing. The video was a huge accomplishment and a step forward for the Dawgz. For the family, it is all we have left of my brother besides memories and pictures. I am so glad that we created the website so that anytime I want to hear my brother's voice, I can. That is priceless. Nik Platinum still carries on the legacy of the Rezawar Dawgz and his solo tracks can be heard on www.rezawardawgz.com and clicking on "dawgtracks".

14

Donny Goes To The Newspaper

Donny had been receiving calls from the *Boston Herald* since the show started, but he always refused their offers to do an interview. He had also received calls from *The National Enquirer* and *TV Guide* who both expressed interest in the rights to this very story! He wouldn't dream of being vindictive to Mark, let alone saying anything about Mark publicly. Those close to Donny told him he was crazy not to do the interviews. He thought he would be betraying Mark by going to the newspapers when, in fact, Mark is the one who betrayed him! He needed to forget about being true to Mark and be more concerned with himself.

Donny knew that if he did the interview, he could probably get the newspapers to mention The Rezawar Dawgz and even plug his website. He had been so hurt by Mark. Naturally, the anger followed. Ultimately, bitterness got the best of him because he called the newspapers to do the interview about *Entourage* and the scandal behind it. The following article was published in the *Boston Herald* on June 5, 2005.

Life's Lonely Outside Wahlberg's '*Entourage*'
When Mark Wahlberg's semi-autobiographical comedy *Entourage* kicks off its second season on HBO tonight (June 5, 2005), Donnie Carroll of Dorchester won't be laughing. That's because Donnie, aka "Donkey," the model for Turtle—the baseball-cap-wearing, Hummer-driving, pot-and-women-wrangling gofer says his old pal Mark hasn't kicked him any *Entourage* cash.

"I've been by his side since Day One," brayed the Donkey. "Ever since his days as Marky Mark. And I got nothing. Not 10 cents. Nothing." Donkey says Wahlberg, whom he's known since they were both teenagers hanging on the corner of Savin Hill and Dorchester Avenue, has taken care of the rest of his crew whom the *Entourage* characters are modeled after. But even though Carroll claims the idea for a show about Hollywood hangers-on was his, he's been cut out.

"He gave me his word that he would take care of me, and I still think he will," Donkey said. "But I'm still waiting." Wahlberg's peeps didn't get back to us to respond. *Entourage,* which premiered on the cable channel last season (2004), is the story of Hollywood up-and-comer Vince Chase, played by preening pretty boy Adrian Grenier and the posse of homeboys he drags along to Tinseltown. There's his brother, Johnny Chase, aka Johnny Drama, a desperate wannabe, hilariously played by Kevin Dillon, real-life bro of actor Matt Dillon. He's based on Wahlberg's "cousin" John Alves, a bodybuilder and washed-up actor whose credits include "Southie," Donnie Wahlberg's 1998 flick, and the "Marky Mark Workout" video.

Alves' real-life nickname is Johnny Drama. Kevin Connolly's sensible manager-in-waiting, Eric, is based on Wahlberg's pal Eric Weinstein, a middle-aged Bronx homey whom the actor met on the set of "The Basketball Diaries," Ari Gold, Vince's foul-mouthed, fast-talking, womanizing bully of an agent played by Jeremy Piven is said to be a send-up of Mark's real-life manager Ari Emanuel. And Turtle, the groupie-groping goofball played by Jerry Ferrara, is based on Donkey, who carried Wahlberg's bags for more than 14 years while trying to launch a career as a rap musician under the name Murder One. "I got paid $500 a week to hang out," Donkey said. "I got paid to live his life."

But while Weinstein is given a producer credit on the series, and Alves is listed as a consultant, Wahlberg hasn't shelled out any *Entourage* dough for the inspiration of Turtle. Before the show debuted, Wahlberg had Donny sign a release that read, in part: "*As you are aware, there is a character in the program presently named 'Turtle.' Although the character is intended to depict a fictional person, the name is similar to your nickname and the character may exhibit certain characteristics that are similar to yours or be involved in certain events that are similar to events that you may be involved in."*

Donkey says he was not paid to sign the release, but that Wahlberg promised he would "be taken care of." In fact, Donkey flew out to Hollywood and auditioned for the role of Turtle. He says the producers loved him, but he lost out when *Entourage* writers decided to make Vince a Queens native. "They said they needed New York actors," Carroll complained. All of which is particularly galling, Donkey says, because he first came up with the idea of a show about an actor's posse. "I told Mark I wanted to do a reality show about me," he said. "I had an idea for a book, too. It was called *From the Hood to Hollywood, A Soldier's Story*. It was about a kid like me who grows up with a kid like Mark and ends up in Hollywood with him livin' the life. But Mark said, 'No one cares about that.' Now look at it!" Carroll, who is unemployed, is still trying to launch a music career with his hip-hop group, *Rezawar Dawgz* (www.rezawardawgz.com), who once opened for 'N Sync.

A few years ago, Wahlberg shot a documentary about the band for a never-produced reality series, another kick in the ass for Donkey. "I got a 14-year-old daughter I gotta support," he said. "When I'm out in Hollywood, he shows me a lot of love, but what's love, taking me out to sushi dinners? What about my daughter?" Donkey says he still hears from Mark whenever the actor is in Boston, and "I still love him like a brother." "But," he says, "it shouldn't have to come down to this. He should do the right thing."

Donny knew he'd crossed the line and that there was certainly no going back now. I loved it! We were all so proud of him. I am tired of idiots trying to make those who are doing the right thing, somehow look bad. Donny was a little upset at how the printed article translated what he said, but he really thought there was a polite way to dance around the truth. I found the article to be concise and basically to the point. I know it bothered him, but he had to do it. It's too bad when someone puts you in that kind of a situation.

I've found that people have much more respect for you when you stand up for yourself. Donny never wanted it to end this way. None of us did. He loved Mark. Who else, in the midst of a dispute like this one, is quoted saying "I love him like a brother?"

It's my brother's big heart and whimsical ways that make me compelled to tell his story. And as soon as this book is done, I will be contacting all the popular media shows in an effort to get the truth out. I won't give up until justice is served.

15

The Official Falling Out

Mark was pissed off when the article came out. Even better, because it came out on his birthday. Nobody likes to take a shot at someone's character, but when you screw them over, you should probably expect some kind of retaliation, especially if you're from Boston!

I believe karma is real. Are you familiar with the saying "what goes around comes around?" I am hoping to be a contributing factor to Wahlberg's fate. To think, in a million years, Mark probably never dreamed anything would come back to bite him. But nobody messes with a Carroll, not if I can help it! I can't wait until people are saying "Did you read that book about the *Entourage* scandal?"

As a matter of fact, I'll be sure to send copies directly to people from our home town where this story really matters most! So that was pretty much the end of Donny's and Mark's long journey together, but not the end of the story. Donny had wanted to write this book himself, only his story was supposed to end with "Mark and him being best buds forever, living the good life." Somehow, only one of them ended up that way while the other was forced to reflect on the last decade of his life.

Everybody in our town was talking about the article. Mutual friends of Donny and Mark would eventually have to choose sides. There were people who stayed loyal to Donny and then there were the wannabe's. They actually thought their loyalty to Wahlberg would somehow pay off. You'd think they wouldn't keep making the same mistake my brother made by trusting someone as greedy as Mark. Hadn't Mark already shown he had no loyalty to his best friend? Unlike Donny, these people are actually comfortable being "Mark's bitches." They continue to hang on to Mark's fame and embrace it as if *they* were living the dream. They're the "wannabe's," at least Donny was an original.

Needless to say, the tension was high, and Donny didn't trust too many people anymore. He tried to brush it off as if it didn't bother him. He continued rapping with a newfound determination and *Rezawar Dawgz* was prepared to start marketing their demo. Everyone familiar with their music knew that quite a few songs were about the *Entourage* scandal. *Dawgz* had made the songs and Donny vented his anger in them, but deep down I don't believe he would have released them at that point. He still clung to the hope that Mark would come forward and honor his word. But that day never came.

No matter how hard he tried to get on with his life, Donny fell deeper into a depression over the whole ordeal. It wasn't just the fact that Mark had knifed him in the back regarding the show, although that was HUGE! But their friendship was officially over! It was the BIG break up. Donny just couldn't move beyond that no matter how he tried.

Donny took it pretty hard. He sulked around and still dwelled on the whole newspaper incident even though we reassured him that he did the right thing. It was like a relationship when one of the partners cheats and the other person is completely devastated. They just don't believe it, or there must be some logical explanation for it. But after some time had passed and Donny had a chance to reflect on the whole situation; he accepted that Mark really did screw him, though he wasn't very forgiving about it. It also bothered him that his close buddies still remained loyal to Mark even though they knew the truth.

One person who stayed true to Donny was Nik Platinum, his rap partner. They tried to promote their album by marketing the website. Who knows what could have been for the *Dawgz* if not for the demise of my brother.

After things cooled down a bit, Donny mustered up the courage to write Walberg a letter about what happened between them, only he never gave it to him. After showing us the letter, we told him he was crazy not to give it to him. Donny was apprehensive about crossing that kind of line with Mark and so he held on to it. This letter would be his final words to Mark Wahlberg. A handwritten letter is included emphasizing exactly what Donny want to say.

DONNY SPEAKS June 2005

Mr. Wahlberg,
You know all you had to do was take care of me like you said and none of this would have even happened. You don't need to be a rocket scientist to figure that out. Even Eric reassured me that if I signed the consent form I would be taken care of. You know it wouldn't have cost you one penny because you could have made HBO take care of me like they did with Cuzin and Eric.

What did 12 years of loyalty and carrying your bag get me? Nothing, zip, zero, big goose egg. That's the reason I'm writing this to you again because I never have the opportunity to talk to you alone. The reason I never see you when you come to Boston is because I feel so much anger built up inside I think it's better if I stay away for now.

I do love you like a brother but I am really hurt by you. I have been loyal to you and always have kept my mouth shut and I always defend you if I have to. It really bothers me when everyone is getting paid off the "Entourage" when the shit way back before it came out was my idea.

Maybe if Beata listed to me and believed in me before shit would have worked. Nobody believed that somebody like me who lives and works for a movie-star would be a big hit but that article was pretty classy if you want to know the truth. The paper twisted it the way they wanted. I didn't say one thing to dis you and you know that.

If I wanted that shit could have been ugly but I have respect for you and maybe now you will for me. Just be honest with me. Deep down in your heart you know it was my idea. I been talking about it for 10 years.

P.S. I want you to know the Herald has been asking me for 2 years now to do an interview and I refused every time until now. She asked me to do an interview on the Entourage and I said no, I said I would do one on Murda 1 and the Rezawar Dawgz if they plugged my site, which they did.

They twisted everything as newspapers usually do. Also she said the article was coming out on Monday, not on your birthday. I yelled at them for that. Also for what it's worth I told them not to dis you. I made myself clear that if they do dis you I would never speak to them again.

I have received calls from TV Guide and the National Enquirer. I refuse to call them because you know the last thing in life, I don't want you to get hurt by something I didn't say. I never said you cheated me out of money. I said I wasn't paid yet but believe you was going to take care of me. I don't regret doing the interview because my website has gotten 1000 hits in 2 days but I do regret them twisting it like they did so I'm sorry if I hurt you.

I contacted Mark and sent him a copy of this letter demanding he do right by my family and cease and desist using the Turtle character since this letter from Donny proves that they did not have permission to use his character for free. He was flat out lied to and told by Wahlberg's manager that "he'd be taken care of."

MR. Wahlberg,

You know all you had to do was make sure I was taking care of like you said and none of this would have even happened. You don't need to be a Rocket-scientest to figure that one out. Even Eric Reassured me that if I signed the consent form I would be taken care of. You know it wouldn't have cost you one penny because you could have made HBO take care of me like they did with cuzin and Eric. What did 12 years of loyalty and carrying your bags got me? nothing, zip, zero, Big goose egg. Thats the reason I'm writing this to you again because I never have the opportunity to talk to you alone. The reason I never see you when you come to Boston is because I feel so much anger built up inside I think its better if I stay away for now I do love you like a brother but I am Really hu by you. I have been loyal to you and always have kept my mouth shut and I always def you if I have to. It really bothers me wh everybody is getting paid off the "Entourage" when the shit was back before it came out was my idea. Maybe if beats listened to and believed in me before shit would have Nobody believed that someone like me who lives a works for a movie star would be a big hit

The Official Falling Out

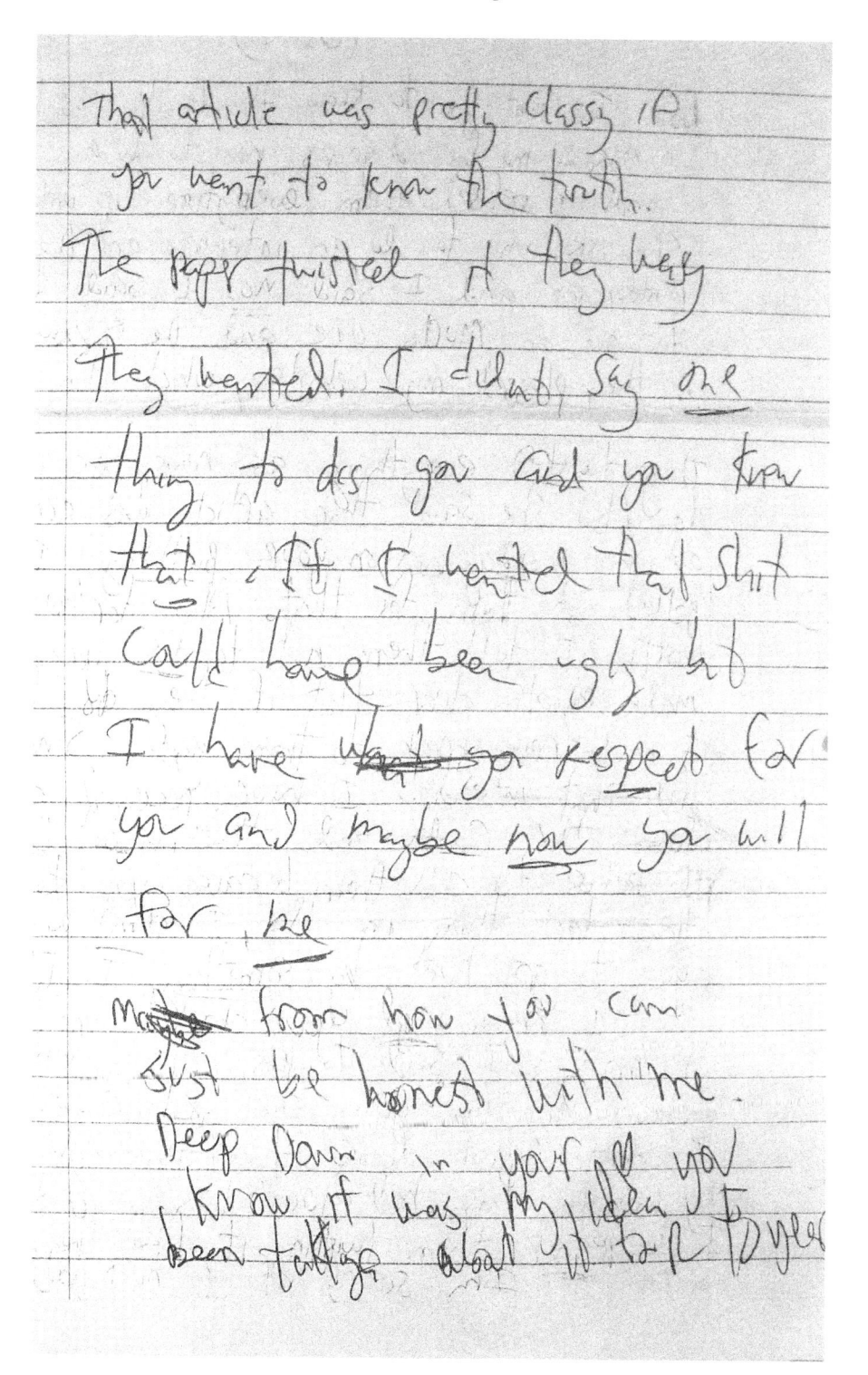

That article was pretty classy if
you want to know the truth.
The paper twisted it they way
they wanted. I didn't say one
thing to diss you and you know
that. If I wanted that shit
could have been ugly but
I have what so respect for
you and maybe now you will
for me

Ma~~ybe~~ from how you can
just be honest with me.
Deep Down in yourself you
know it was my ~~when you
been telling~~ about it to R Tyler

16

December 18th

December 18, 1999 was the anniversary with my "then, boyfriend," now husband. It was the date we first kissed We had been good friends for two years. After college, we started our business, 1218 Productions.

On December 17, 2005, we were getting ready for bed. It was around 11:30. We had set our alarm for 12:18 am, just after midnight, our official sixth anniversary. I knew he had a special gift for me. We were going to sleep for a little while and wake up to open it, then go back to sleep. That was the plan. (yeah, I know…corny).

Anyway, it didn't quite go as planned. Instead, my cell phone rang. I was puzzled because nobody ever called this late. Everyone I usually talked to in Boston would be asleep by now. By the time I found my phone, it had stopped ringing and my house phone was ringing. Suddenly, I thought it had to be my sister since she just had a baby ten days before. In that split second, I assumed she was probably up late with the baby and thought she'd try me. That had to be it! But as quickly as the thought could process in my brain, my boyfriend's cell phone rang. From across the hall we looked at each other with a look of… I don't know… confusion? I glanced at our clock which read 11:30pm, and in my head I did the math. "Twelve-thirty, one-thirty, two- thirty!" Two-thirty! Right away I thought about my brother. "Something happened, I know it!"

Jeff tossed the phone to me. That moment was surreal. The call was coming from my sister's house. I knew she would NEVER call my boyfriend's phone, unless of course…in case of an emergency.

My heart pounded. My brother had been in the hospital on Friday night, just one night before, due to, yet again, another one of his bad asthma attacks. I brought the phone to my ear and I'll never forget how the conversation went. Expecting my sister's voice, I was caught off guard yet again, as my father's voice came through the receiver.

"Debbie, this is your father."

And I was thinking…'yeah, I know your voice Dad, but why the hell are you at Nina's house (my sister) at 2:30 in the morning?' But what I actually said was …"Dad? Don't tell me what I know you're going to tell me."

I said that sentence three times in a row as he silently listened on the other end. He could have been calling about anything. Something could have happened to anyone in the family, but I KNEW when my boyfriend's phone rang that Donny was gone. I KNEW IT!

I can only assume this knowledge came from Donny himself. I used to think having psychic ability meant "I had a gift," but after reading many books on spiritual communication, I knew it was Donny who made me aware. The messages we receive come from spirits.

As I write this part, I'm fighting back a river of tears. My father never even had to say my brother's name, neither one of us did. Being used to Donny's frequent bouts with death, we always knew this day could come. But I simply said…"Don't tell me what I know you're going to tell me." When he finally spoke, all he said was…"It's happened…it's happened."

I literally went down to my knees. My dogs ambushed me with attention. Dogs are very empathetic, any dog person knows this. My sister later told me that she could hear me crying and screaming over the phone. I was 3000 miles away and never got to see him alive again. I couldn't help remembering just two months earlier, when I could tell for the first time in the nine years I'd been in California, that my brother actually missed me. "When you moving back?" He said with a distinct Boston attitude.

I left for the airport that day. October 16, 2005. The last day I saw my brother alive. I remembered telling my significant other when I got back to Cali, how hard it was to be so far from my family, and that even my brother missed me! Donny had a big heart, but he didn't wear it on his sleeve. I could not believe it was real; that I was never going to see him again.

When I regained my composure, I told my father I would get a flight immediately and we hung up. The rest was a little vague to me. We never even said his name. I just knew he was gone.

That night, I refused to sleep in my bed. I was gripped with that fear we all get when we first hear that someone close to us has died. Many of you know exactly what I'm talking about. It really hits home when you lose one of your family. I stared at my Christmas tree that night. The twinkling lights turned different parts of the tree into a rainbow of beauty. Suddenly, it meant nothing. Everything felt like a movie. How the hell could I fathom Christmas at all? We slept on the floor beside the tree that night because I was afraid to be in my room. I needed the superficial distortion of reality that night.

It had to be worse for my sister—being there, live, and in person. Of course, I'd have given anything to be there, no matter how hard it was. None of them got to see him alive; he was gone before we even knew about it. My sister hadn't stepped foot out of her house in ten days. She had just given birth to her first child on December 7, and like most new mothers, was not in a hurry to go out in the bitter winter coldness.

She had turned her cell ringer off earlier than usual because of the new baby. She awoke later in the night with a strange feeling, and for some reason felt compelled to get out of bed, creep down stairs, and check the phone. As she scrolled the caller ID, she gasped when she noticed a dozen or so missed calls, most from my brother's own cell phone. Some of the calls were from the niece of my brother's landlord who happened to be more than a family friend to us.

Panic stricken, my sister stood there shaking all over as she frantically dialed my brother's phone. It was my brother's girlfriend Maria who answered. "What the hell happened!" my sister shouted in a panic.

Through tears the girl delivered the dreaded news. "Donny passed away."

Those words would ring in my sister's ears for weeks and months to come. Her husband was home that night and was able to stay home with the baby. She grabbed the car keys and raced out into the winter air, pajamas and all, and drove to the hospital. Her husband worried as he watched her go. He was left alone to deal with the shock of our brother's death by himself. The scene she described will haunt me forever.

When she got to the hospital, my father was standing over Donny. His hands were in his pocket and his head was hung low, as if staring at the floor. He could barely stand to look at his son. It was all too unreal. My mother was so devastated that she waited outside the room. She couldn't, wouldn't…dream of seeing her son like that. My sister rushed into my mother's arms. My mother tried to console her. I remember my sister telling me that she was surprised that my mother didn't drop dead herself since her worst nightmare had come true. Our mother was the kind of person who worried about everything you can imagine, so my sister was caught off guard by her uncharacteristic strength during what had to have been a terrible shock and the worst day of her life.

My sister went back into the room and stood beside my dad. The two of them embraced and together said their silent goodbyes.

We assumed his death was asthma related. It had to be. He'd been in and out of the hospital an average of three or four times each year of his entire life. We found out that he checked himself out of the hospital early the night before. My last conversation with him was on Friday night, just a day before his death. Who knew this conversation would be the last time I ever spoke to my brother? I remember the whole thing as if it were yesterday.

"Donny, do you want to die?" I asked.

"No!" He answered quickly.

"Then the dog has to go!"

"You know me, I would NEVER give up a dog, but it's not worth dying over." Donny's dog Diesel was a 150 pound mastiff. He was tan with a black muzzle and Donny, much like myself, tended to regard dogs as 'better than human.' This dog was his baby! Of course, he had his daughter, but animal people understand that specific bliss that can only come from being loved by a dog.

He told me he had talked to his boss, a guy he was doing odd jobs for, who had offered to take Diesel. He said Donny could come and take the dog for walks and outings any time. I told him that he was so lucky. I mean, how often do you find someone great to take a dog and get visitation rights, too? He said he was happy about it, but still sad that they wouldn't be living together anymore. He would lie in bed and sleep with his arm wrapped around the gigantic dog. Diesel could do no wrong in his eyes.

I told him that he better get some rest and I would call tomorrow. I always told the people in my family I loved them. I started saying it long ago because I always wanted them to know that I loved them in case there was ever a question. Life gives you a different perspective when you're 3000 miles from those you love.

"Love ya," I said.

"Love ya, too," he replied.

And you can bet not a day goes by that I don't thank God for the chance to have those final words. Some people aren't so lucky.

We were all in shock. Mark Wahlberg was the last person in our minds during that time. We knew about the falling out, of course. But that didn't matter. We never had any serious gripe with Mark because we always believed he would ultimately do right by Donny. I wholeheartedly believed that. Honest to God! But as time went by, Mark's true colors emerged.

17

Gold Diggers

Christmas week is the worst time for someone to die. It's just the worst. I spent Christmas week meeting with the funeral home listening to a non-chalant version of funeral protocol as we made the final arrangements. I was still in a daze, hardly able to even conceive that this had really happened to my family. At the same time, I knew it was happening. Unless you've been through it, you can't even imagine what it's like. It's even more shocking when the person who died was only 39 with a life full of promise.

I was heartbroken for us all, especially my niece and our parents. My sister was crushed. The birth of her child would be forever tainted with this dark memory. It was pretty hard to celebrate anything. I was strong, but I needed to be stronger for everyone else. It was the new baby, that God sent eleven days before, that would ultimately save us all from the brink of devastation. As sad as I was, it was bittersweet. I couldn't do anything but smile when I laid eyes on this perfect angel.

It should come as no surprise, that the women from my brother's past— both his ex-girlfriend, and his current girlfriend, ransacked his apartment looking for money. All of a sudden our family was thrown headfirst into a whirlwind of meaningless drama that we wanted nothing to do with. It got so bad that I asked my uncle Jack, a retired police officer, to arrange to have a few patrol cars outside the funeral home in the event of an incident. The funeral was still a few days off, but already I was fit to be tied. This was the last thing I thought I'd be dealing with. I was still trying to wrap my head around the reality that Donny was gone.

We were all so consumed with this "girlfriend drama" that we barely had time to grieve his death! Nobody knows what these idiots put us through. Their greedy, selfish antics were sickening. People were attacking us at every angle about money. My brother's gold-digging girlfriend, actually had the audacity to accuse my sister and father of taking money out my dead brother's pockets! She was way out of line. At least, our family worked for a living instead of sponging off everyone else. She was lucky she stayed clear of me or it was going to get VERY ugly. Then my niece's mother called telling me, that according to his daughter, Donny had $16,000.00 hidden in the ceiling of his bedroom. Like I give a shit? My brother is dead and you're talking about money?

Are we supposed to go to my brother's house, find the money, and then hand it over to her? Thank God my parents had life insurance on him because it cost close to $17,000 to send him off in style. If there had been that kind of money lying around, it should have helped pay for Donny's funeral arrangements, since it was Donny's money. These dirt bags didn't give a shit about my family's pain. Strangely, the mystery money never surfaced. I'm sure someone in that house knows what really happened. Someone always knows. There was way too much drama over the mystery money, so there might have been some truth to it.

This girlfriend of his took everything he owned including his jeep, his computer system, which had all the elite sound-making software, and all the accessories. Donny was a rapper, so when it came to equipment, he had it all. My family didn't care. We assumed all his valuables would go to his daughter anyway, so we stayed out of it. We figured, if they wanted to act like animals, we would let them fight it out among themselves. Luckily, my father was able to go to my brother's apartment to salvage a few items for us to keep. We never got the chance to clean out his things because his house was torn apart long before we had a chance to get there. The funny part is that some of Donny's friends had the audacity to talk about my family. I actually find it amusing how stupid and shallow people are. One friend said to my sister..."Everybody thinks you guys are being mean to Maria."

Little do they know what a manipulative phony she is, and being bipolar, can't possibly help the situation any. I could care less what people thought. They had no idea what had been going on between us, and I wasn't about to explain it to anyone. When my brother's daughter asked her what happened to the money, this greedy bitch said to her "Why don't you ask your aunt and grandfather?"

From my perspective, it seemed as if the only people who really cared that Donny died were me, my sister, my parents, our extended family, and a few close friends.

So I had words with her because I didn't buy into her bullshit. She's lucky that's all she had with me, because it could have gotten really ugly. You know what they say…you can take the girl out of the schoolyard, but you can't take the schoolyard out of the girl, especially a Dorchester girl. Within months of my brother's death, she was shacking up with a friend of his a few towns over which just proves what a floozie she was to begin with.

During the previous summer, we were at my brother's house for his daughter's birthday party when I noticed her flashing a ring in everyone's face. I pulled my brother aside and asked him, "Are you really going to marry her?"

"Probably," he said.

Now I'm not sure what the rest of the world thought, and I'm sure she put on a show for Donny's friends, but one thing my family knew for sure was that he was NOT in love with her. We had seen him in love before, and what he had with this girl was far from love. He wasn't surprised or even insulted when I asked him, as a matter of fact, he laughed.

So I asked, "Then, why?"

My father was there during this discussion. In the end, his answer was that he would marry her because he wasn't getting any younger. I think he knew he would be settling, but at least he'd be getting laid! My father and I cracked up laughing, and quite honestly, you can't hold that against anyone, especially a man. He's a man! They need sex as much as they can get it! Even I know that!

We all knew there had to be an ulterior motive because he certainly didn't love her. He made that pretty clear. He confided in us more than some of his friends when it came to real stuff. He was actually talking to his daughter's mother shortly before his death. I remember my niece said to me the same day, that "My mother and father might get back together."

"Oh," was all I could manage to say, considering she wasn't exactly a step in the right direction either. My brother was only a bank to these females.

Maria was quick to take the liberty of notifying the press of my brother's death, even before we knew the cause of death for sure, therefore setting off a media frenzy of articles that read "Real-Life Turtle Dies." She was not family, never was, nor ever would be (thank God), and had no right to do that. My family's privacy was violated by this greedy gold-digger who hoped to profit at the expense of my brother's death.

The whole thing between Maria and me began two months earlier. She told me that she and my brother were planning a trip to visit me in California. I was at my sister's new house for the first time when she and Donny stopped by. She was rambling on and on, when suddenly I cut her off…"You don't think you're coming to visit me without my niece do you?"

"Well, uh… we thought…."

I basically "blew her hair back" and pretty much told her that for years I had begged them to bring my niece for a visit. She had always wanted to go to California. And now, she was telling me that they were going to come to California without my niece? We argued, and in the end, this is exactly what she said to me. Only she was hysterical now, as tears started shooting out of her in all directions. I felt like a man caught in the moment, when that sudden shock that comes over you, when women cry. She screamed like a psychopath in the middle of the street… "Alright, I hate my life! Is that what you want to know? I hate my life! I hate my life with your brother!"

I really didn't want to know that, but I guess she was going to tell me anyway. As ruthless as I can be at times, I started laughing at her. I think it was because I just couldn't believe that she was crying over absolutely nothing! She clearly had no experience with confrontation. All I wanted was for them to bring my niece for a visit, but she turned it into a federal case. Who even asked her about her life with Donny? Then I got in my car and left to ensure I didn't end up at the police station because if I stayed any longer it could have gotten even worse. She was still crying and screaming in the street as we drove off.

I remembered that day at the cookout, when Maria flashed that same ring in my sister's face. She was smiling ear-to-ear. My sister looked at her as serious as a heart attack and said "You don't think he'll ever marry you, do you?"

Her happiness quickly turned to a look of utter disappointment. The funny thing was I used to be nice to her until I noticed she was using my brother and telling me she hated her life with him.

"You hate your life?" I said that day. "Hit the fucking road…leave him! Be responsible for your own damn happiness!" I shouted.

But what I really wanted to say was "PLEASE, do us the favor, and hit the road!"

She was going overboard. These days, and even then, I knew enough to walk away from trouble. I knew myself, too well, to know that if I didn't walk away, I could very likely end up in jail. Some people never liked me because I tell it like it is – the reason for this book. On the contrary, many others liked me for that very same reason.

This bitch was complaining she hated her life and it sucked. After all the money Donny spent on her! Jewelry… dinners out every night! Nothing was ever good enough for her! He always had a roll of cash, and spent a lot of it to "shut her up" as he put it once.

I never told him about the spat, but apparently, she did. My sister was discussing it on the phone with my brother the very same night while I sat right beside her.

"I don't know what they were fighting about," she said as we exchanged glances.

He didn't know I was sitting there. He also didn't want me to know that he even knew about it. So he and I never discussed it. We had a very good relationship and respected each other. I don't go out of my way to defend my opinion. If people pass judgment without knowing the facts, then their opinion don't matter.

18

Saying Goodbye

After days of pure hell, and Jerry Springer-like episodes, we gathered at our neighborhood's notorious Murphy's Funeral Home in Dorchester, Massachusetts to say goodbye to Donny Carroll, my only brother, aka "Donkey," aka "Murder One." He was many things to many people. Friends and relatives began pouring in, and with them came plenty of funny "Donny" stories. I even found myself laughing a few times. There was no way you couldn't laugh when talking about Donny. He was pure comedy. I remained solid as a rock that day, we all did. Then, shortly after it all began, my mother pulled me aside and asked, "It's going to be alright…isn't it?"

She surprised even herself with this newfound strength, as most of us do, when faced with something like this. What other choice do you have? I love this one quote from *The Shawshank Redemption*, when Andy says, "Get busy living or get busy dying."

It really comes down to that. What choice do you have? I cherish life more than most people because I know how fleeting it can be. This is why I choose to be strong and positive instead of dwelling on things that can't be changed.

So, we held our heads high that day and sucked it up. We settled on a closed casket; it was hard enough without seeing Donny in a coffin. The person never looks like themselves. It may be a tradition, but you can see why some traditions are modified every few centuries. A funeral is not an easy thing for a family to go through, besides we're a very private family. My niece asked us to leave the casket open, although we were against it. We agreed though, that for her sake, we would. Now we had to be even stronger. I don't know about you, but my heart pounds when I go to funerals. But this would, after-all, be the last time she would see her father forever. Some people who came were caught off guard because they were expecting the casket to be closed.

My eyes were glued to the entrance of the room the whole time and my adrenaline pumped as I waited to see who would show up. My hope was that there would be no drama. I waited and wondered if Maria would have the audacity to start trouble. Nothing surprised me at this point. She was becoming more unpredictable by the day. But I had my police back-up close by, just in case. I stood there staring at my brother. I kept saying inside…"How could you leave us with this mess?"

There was no doubt that my brother knew a lot of people. As they started to come in, I found myself doing the consoling, rather than the one being consoled. I was standing in front of him, alone, and could hear loud sobbing behind me. I turned around to see Maria standing there. Our eyes met. I remained composed. She looked up at me, and actually reached her arms out to hug me. Slobbering and sobbing, she said, "I'm sorry."

Of course, I didn't hug her back.

"I'm sorry, too," was all I managed before turning and giving her the notorious flip of the hair.

Cruel as many of you may think I am, I'm not phony. This girl was a gold-digger, and she knew it better than anyone. Furthermore, she knew that I knew it. So, am I supposed to be a fake and hug her for the sake of impressions? I see things as they are, and call people out, when necessary, while most people look the other way.

My mind was racing as I was still trying to piece together what really happened the night my brother died. We had heard through the grapevine that Maria waited a long time before calling an ambulance. She later told us, "He didn't want to go to the hospital!"

This is an example of why I wanted to rip her head off. "He didn't want to go?" If there was one thing that my mother drilled into everybody's head, who came within three feet of my brother, was that you can never let him make that decision. So, while he was in the bathroom…dying…she was in the living room playing video games! We were also informed that the ambulance was given the wrong address, therefore, driving aimlessly around until they were able to get the right information. People wonder why I'm bitter towards her…why I wanted to smack her across her ugly face? Because she could have saved my brother's life that night! She even said so herself while recanting the night events… "He was in there a long time."

I couldn't believe what I was hearing, and it just kept getting worse. My family was reeling with the death alone, and now, all of this new information was surfacing. It was the on-sight landlord at the residence, who happened to be an old friend of my parents, who called the ambulance that night. She told my parents to "get to the hospital asap." That's all she said. She later told a mutual friend of my mothers "A lot of mistakes were made that night."

We never gave that information to my mother or my niece. That mutual friend was like my second mother, so she told me directly. Imagine how my sister and I felt when we heard this? Things were bad enough already. We had enough drama, as it was, without opening yet another can of worms. I can't blame her for his death, but if she had just half a brain, my brother might still be alive today. Our grieving process was interrupted by greedy idiots, so yeah… I could care less if people thought "we were being mean to her."

My mother told me that Donny confided in her, that Maria had slapped him in the face many times, and that she was always asking for money. He just blamed it on her being bipolar and was used to her frequent bouts of rage. He told my mother that she was always flipping out and crying all the time. She was riding his shirt tails hoping for the fame and fortune, too.

None of us could understand why the hell he stayed with her. We didn't like that she used him, plain and simple, the same way many of the judgmental wannbe's used him to try to get to Mark.

People filled the funeral home. Some of my brother's friends who came in actually gave us dirty looks. They didn't even have the decency to come through the family line to pay their respects. I remember my sister pulling me aside.

"What's the deal with them?" she said, as my eyes followed the direction of her nod.

"I don't know," I replied, as I stared back at them, puzzled by their obvious attitudes.

I honestly have no idea why some of my brother's "so called friends" snubbed us at the service, but I am left to speculate that his girlfriend probably told them we weren't acknowledging her, and that we were mean etc…boo, fucking, hoo! What she failed to tell them was all of the shit she said about my brother right before he died. I wonder what the police would have thought had they known that "she hated her life with my brother" and then he ends up dying a week later? Have you ever watched *20/20*? Isn't there usually an investigation when someone dies? Is it a crime to not call 911 in a timely manner? It should be! So I can't worry about what people think when they don't know the real story. What right does anyone have to judge us when they don't have a clue what they are talking about! I can only go by what I know is fact.

My brother was very close to his family and these people have the nerve to look at my family condescendingly? If anything, some of these assholes came to pay *disrespect,* rather than respect. I was certain this arrogance had nothing to do with Wahlberg, because at this point, the falling out was in the early stages, and what did my family have to do with it then? We had faith in Mark; I actually expected him to walk in at any minute. When I got a break from talking to dozens of people, I took a moment by myself and stared at the flowers that surrounded my brother. I have to admit that the most beautiful arrangement came from Wahlberg himself. It simply read "One Love." I'll never forget; it was a solid white wreath. It was truly the nicest funeral arrangement I'd ever seen. My family was so wrapped up in the death that we never thought of anything *Entourage* related. It just wasn't the time or the place.

Earlier, we talked among ourselves, and were fully prepared to see Mark at the funeral. I admit we were probably just as nervous about seeing him as he was about seeing us, but we agreed that we would simply thank him for coming. We had no intention of bringing anything up and we were not sure what he may have thought, but as the night rolled on, and the crowds began to fade, there was no sign of him anywhere. Many people asked us…"Is Mark here yet?"

My father would occasionally glance at his watch and look towards the entrance. I knew who he was looking for. He was starting to look pissed and commented a few times about the fact that Mark was still a no show. Up til then, my family still had some respect for Mark. But when we knew for certain, that he was not coming, it became a whole new ball of wax. I knew he didn't come because he and my brother had been fighting about the show. As we shook our heads and cursed Wahlberg, my mother came over to us all upset.

"What's the matter?" I asked?

She had held it together all day, so I knew this was different… something or someone had upset her.

She went on to tell us that Mark's manager, Eric, had come over to her when the rest of us were scattered all over the place, and said this to her. These were his exact words as she quoted them to me that day…"I'm sorry for your loss, Mrs. Carroll, but the show was not your son's idea."

As I relive that moment, my adrenaline pumps and my heart beats faster. I can't help it! No matter how hard I try to "talk myself into remaining calm," I just want to explode. What went through my mother's mind after he said that? Flabbergasted by his outrageous lie, my mother pulled away from him to find us. My father was so mad after she told us what happened that I had to stop him and my brother-in-law from going after that clown. It surprises me that Jerry Springer didn't get wind of this story because it was turning into quite the show. I had never laid eyes on this creep before and wouldn't know him if I ever bumped into him. I was fit to be tied!

You can bet that if *Entourage* wasn't on our minds before, it certainly was after that comment. Why on earth would he say something like that? Oh, how I wished he had said it to me! This was the first time we heard that they were claiming the show was not Donny's idea? That meant they were calling him a liar when he had talked about this show since the start of Marks career, well over a decade before! Everyone who knew them, knew it because my brother never shut up about it. I always wondered if Mark knew Eric said that to my mother.

I can understand that he was apprehensive about facing us; he had no idea what to expect. My brother had just died during Christmas week! The show was the farthest thing from our minds. This man had the utmost disrespect to dare say such a thing, and what was worse, to just outright lie about it. It is a lie, it can't be true. My family always felt that Eric was the driving force behind this whole scandal between Mark and Donny. Prior to my brother's death, there was still hope that Mark would "take care of him" like he promised. But then my brother died, and boom…problem solved! Or so they thought.

That day I vowed I would get the truth out in the open for my brother. I am telling his story because it is the right thing to do. Are some people going to hate me because I told the truth? My loyalty lies with my family, not the general public or the wannabes. Donny deserves credit. He deserves justice. HBO, along with Mark Wahlberg and Eric Weinstein, stole my brother's intellectual property and actually believe they will get away with it. They really think I am out of their league. Nobody is untouchable. This book will always be associated with the show *Entourage,* and that, in itself, is enough for me.

There is no excuse that someone rich and famous, who can charter a private jet, could POSSIBLY miss his "best friend's" funeral. But Mark never came. Instead, we were left to assume that he sent Eric to relay the message. Were we supposed to say, "Oh, okay…?"

Since when was it not Donny's idea? Oh, I see, my brother is dead now, so this was their weak attempt to set the record straight. It all made sense to me now why Mark sent this dirt-bag in place of himself. He didn't know what to expect from Donny's family and was clearly afraid to face us in person. He is the biggest coward I know. His absence spoke volumes. Everyone we knew couldn't believe he hadn't come! If the show were, in fact, Mark's idea, why would he be afraid to face Donny's family? He actually thought he could cover his tracks with fancy flowers and a "stand-in" to be disrespectful, rather than to pay respect, to his friend and family?

What's even worse is that someone can be so low as to disrespect the deceased at his own damn funeral? At least, wait until he's in the ground, for God's sake! I mean seriously? What a fucking weasel!

After the services, we headed to church for the funeral mass. This meant we were getting that much closer to really losing him forever. At least in church, I knew he was still there. A dear friend of my parent's read a really nice poem called, "I'm Spending Christmas With Jesus This Year." As beautiful as it was, it ripped at my heart. It just felt wrong to be having a funeral on December 22. The church was decorated for the Christmas season which made the whole thing so unreal.

As the crowds filed out of church, we climbed into the back of the family limousine. I'll never forget the feeling of riding in that limousine. I specifically remember getting off at the exit for Cedar Grove cemetery. It was one of those moments that I truly felt as if I were somewhere else. Everything seemed to play out in slow motion. It was so beautiful and peaceful at the grave site. Since it was winter, the ground was like concrete. I took a few long-stemmed red roses from his grave to keep. My sister and I took them to dry, so we could keep them forever. I removed the gold lettering that read "brother" from our floral arrangements. I took one for my sister and one for myself. Just a little something to hold on to. The only good thing was that Donny would be buried in the very same row as his friend Jason. It was a fairly new section in the cemetery, so we specifically asked for that row. We knew that my brother would have wanted that. We also felt he was with Jason now.

I stood there on the frozen ground, my heart as cold as the weather. Sometimes I wished it was all over, though at other times, I wished it would never end. They say the easy part is when all the people are around to support you. But the hardest part is after they all leave and you have to start life over again, without that person, without my brother.

The only peace I got was when I was alone at night. But even then, it really wasn't peaceful. My mind raced, and replayed everything I'd lived through in the past week. It was so sickening; I felt nauseous for days and days. Anyone who's been through this knows that you just go into a survival mode and instinct just kicks in.

I was so scared every night. Death has a strange way of putting things into perspective. I imagined how life would have been if this had never happened. When I awoke each morning, the first thing I always hoped for was that it was all a bad dream. It just couldn't have happened! But it did. I would pray for sleep to consume me and take me far away from this nightmare my family was living in. I am writing now how scared I was and how alone I felt, but at the time, I put on a good show. I felt detached from the situation, but my internal defense mechanisms were forcing me to go on. I was stronger than I thought I was. Always listen to your primitive instincts. I am good at "holding it together" when I have to. Or, at least, looking like I'm OK. It helped so much to have the support of friends and family, and we are thankful to everyone who came to pay their respects to my brother.

To this day, I am still in denial. Of course, I know it happened. Of course, I know he's gone. But I just can't bring myself to really believe it. I just block it out instead, which many people tell me is not healthy, but I feel as though living through it was bad enough.

19

Left Behind

How could I possibly concentrate on work when I had just buried my brother a week ago? I flew back and forth to Boston every three months for years and was pretty accustomed to frequent goodbyes. I truly know the meaning of living a double life. Aside from the usual visits with the family, I always had to get my "Boston food" right away. Unless you've been away from Boston food, you don't know what it's like to go without it. California doesn't have the same kind of pizza or Chinese food that we have on the East coast. So it was necessary to get my pizza and Chinese food on the same day I landed. My mother always used to say … "All she cares about is food."

They laughed at me, but I didn't care. Noone understood! Those are the good memories that make me laugh and, thank God, we have tons of those. Everyone in my family has a good sense of humor. My brother was the funniest person I knew, so you can imagine what my parents were like. I always thought that it was rare that we were all funny. It broke my heart, once again, to leave them, only now it was much worse than before. I never get emotional until they walk away. It rips my heart out every time. I'm almost afraid to leave anyone because you just never know. The toughest part of all was being so far away from my family during that time. At least my parents and sister had each other for support. I wanted to stay to longer than ten days to comfort them and grieve with them, but I had a job and had to get back to work.

Back in California, I stared at the lines ringing on the phone in my office. I was in no mood to work ,and especially, in no mood to be screamed at by angry debtors. I was working in asset recovery for an auto finance company at the time and had the joy of handling the reinstatements. I had many angry callers who wanted their cars back. I hated this work. I wanted to go home and stay for a month. Nobody could cover my position because I was the only one the company wanted handling reinstatements, so I had DOZENS of calls to return. One day, following one of my frequent trips back home, I had 55 messages. So, not only was it hell to come back, I was coming back to hell!

I just wasn't ready to face the world, and I was getting tired of all the pity people were throwing at me. I know they meant well, but I wanted just one day to pass without someone reminding me that my brother was gone. I constantly had to reassure people that we were all doing fine; or at least that's how it looked on the outside. I wanted to talk to people, but they always misunderstood and felt pity. Unless I'm talking to someone close to me, I generally keep my grief to myself. At the same time, it saddened me that time went on. I worried that people would forget about my brother.

At least, in California I didn't have to walk into familiar places every day. I could imagine what the rest of my family went through. Wherever they went, people who had known my brother, would bring it up. My sister would duck away from people at the mall and around the neighborhood just to avoid the subject. At times, she couldn't even escape it when she went to the dentist or to doctor appointments.

Days passed and no matter how hard I tried to give my mind the mental break it deserved, all my free 'mind time' was spent on what that jerk had said to my mother at the funeral. I couldn't get my mother's voice out of my head and what Eric had said to her. It made me so, so mad! I just couldn't believe the audacity of this...jerk! He really thought that by "claiming the idea was not Donny's," that would somehow make it true? Oh, is that how it works? Wahlberg had never verbally claimed the show was his idea until then. He just goes along with the lie now because that's what happens when you're in too deep. It's called the point of no return. This is the same reason he can't look me or my family in the eye: the reason he wrote off Donny's family.

The bottom line is, either he's lying or I'm lying, and boy, would I love to have him take a lie detector test. That's a great idea! Hey, it is a crime, after all. Just another form of corporate, white-collar bullshit! They legally screw people and make lots of money doing it. People think Mark is so great! He sure has a lot of people fooled, and for a while he had me fooled, too! But he's is, after all, an actor.

In the back of my mind, I always thought about contacting him. I couldn't even get the traditional "Thank you" card to him because the wannabes refused to give me the address. Rather, I was told they could "get something to him." Wasn't he Donny's closest friend? Why on earth would they keep his address a secret from Donny's sister? My family never breathed the word "entourage." Why was Walhberg hiding from us? Unless, of course, for obvious reasons. It wasn't too hard to find his address online.

I vowed to myself that it was not over. The funeral was still so recent, yet our family had divided feelings. I felt one way and the rest of the family thought that I was jumping the gun. All I could see was the stone-cold truth. He never contacted us, and I wasn't about to cause more stress for my family. I was tired of pushing the issue and decided to let it go for a while. But I couldn't let Eric get away with what he said, and that's why I wanted to confront Mark. It's almost like he was expecting this all along, and he should expect it! Before that comment, we all thought Mark would make good on his word to Donny or at the very least take care of his orphaned daughter.

I don't even know if Mark knows about that comment. Even though it seemed like Eric was the puppet master, we had already given Wahlberg the benefit of the doubt. Now, I was pretty much done cutting him slack.

We believed that Mark was aware that my niece was orphaned. How could he not know? He knew the intimate details of Donny's life better than anyone, and especially where the concept of the show had come from. Come on now! There was even rumor that Mark was planning on giving her some kind of royalties. I laughed when I heard that, knowing it was bullshit. It was no surprise that the money never came. But he owed her big time. Sadly she was so young at the time, and involved in her own life, that she really didn't know the full extent of the story or what she was even entitled to. The very least he could do, since he stiffed her father out of millions, was to throw her a bone or two. But he did absolutely NOTHING!

It amazes me that he is so quick to donate to multiple organizations around Boston, a place he claims to be so proud of. He doesn't deserve to be associated with Boston; he refers to it as "a ghetto." I wonder if all his Dorchester friends know that he refers to our home town that way?

Dorchester is where we were all from, and if it was a ghetto, just take a look at Wahlberg's criminal past to see how he helped create that reputation. There are many people I know who are proud of where they come from. Many of them may have some kind of criminal record, so I'm not pointing fingers. I'm just saying, don't forget where you come from. You see, this way he gets to keep up his phony persona like the rest of the fakes in Beverly Hills. Yet, he does nothing for Donny's only child? Everyone we associated with thought that was the lowest blow of all. She was just a kid, for God's sake! He must think that everyone believes he is this great big movie star, and I am here to tell you not to judge a book by its cover.

Since my niece's mother was not her legal guardian, and my brother was gone, she was thrown into the system. My parents did their best to be her guardians, but she was a typical teenager, and a little more than they could handle. My sister took her in for a short time, but a newborn and a teenager aren't really a good mix. I wanted to take her all along, but I knew she would never leave her boyfriend to come to California. I was sixteen once, and felt ready for the challenge. I knew I could give her a good chance at life. I offered to take her in and was excited at the prospect. All of my friends warned me "Do you know what you're getting yourself into?" I told them I knew what I was doing. I had been a troubled teenager once and could relate to her. I used to love taking her to the mall and to Chucky Cheese when she was younger. Everywhere we went people would gasp at "how much she looked like her mommy," and I would have to constantly correct people and tell them "I'm her auntie." I would just smile and imagine she was mine for a moment.

But now, here we were, and she had nowhere to go. I was not about to let Donny's only child live on the streets. My husband was supportive. So we worked with the system and got screened to make sure we were potentially good guardians. I wanted her! I even talked to my husband about taking her younger brother, too, who had a different biological father. (also deceased) It just broke my heart that these kids had no stability in their lives. Her brother was extremely fond of Donny; my brother had treated him like his own. Donny adored kids. They reminded him of the innocence we lose when the reality of age sets in.

So here I am, turning my life upside down for this kid, and she goes running around telling everyone, that my family was "making her go to California," and painted us as the bad guys? The irony is that we were the only ones who stepped up to take her. It was quite insulting and worse than a slap in the face. I didn't see anyone from her mother's side of the family step up to take her. For some reason, we were always the bad guys, when all my family ever did was try to do the right thing by her.

For a while, she tried to hide, and then one day, some stupid girl we vaguely knew from years ago, called my mother on the phone. She started giving my mother an earful about what's best for my niece and why we shouldn't make her go to California. My mother had no clue who this idiot was, but a whole other can of worms was falling into our laps. It was my niece's choice all along, and for the record, she pissed me off so badly, because of what this drama was doing to everyone else, that I told her "Forget it, the deal's off." Within weeks, she was begging me to reconsider. She called me up asking me to go through with the background check. She was telling everyone different stories, playing us all against each other.

When my sister got wind of this, she called that girl who had called my mother, and ripped her head off. She ended the call by telling this nosy girl that this was family business, and since she wasn't family, she better mind her own damn business. My sister also told her that if she called my mother again, it wasn't going to be pretty. Of course, the girl was stunned, and stuttered over her own words. Needless to say, that put an end to that. If my brother only knew the hell he left us in. WE did nothing to deserve this.

My niece stayed in a foster home for a while, and they were kind enough to take her brother, too. While staying there, she agreed to come to California on a trial basis. She came for five days and actually loved it. Although she didn't come to live with me permanently, I hoped we would remain close.

She went back to Boston and then disappeared for a year. We knew where she was and that she was safe. We knew she would hate us if we turned her in. My sister told her straight up… "You're sixteen-years old, there is not going to be a search party if you disappear."

We knew she was fine and happier bouncing around from friend to friend. It was too bad that she severed contact with us then because we were the only family of her father left in this world. My family did everything in our power to give her a chance at a better life, but she chose to stay with a boyfriend who cheated on her. If she only knew how much more she deserved. This guy never deserved her in the first place, and still doesn't. I hope one day, when she's had enough, she will come to her senses. When you're young, you don't listen to advice. You have to live and learn. That is the only way you can better your life. She ultimately surfaced after her eighteenth birthday. She had written her whole family off for more than a year of her life. We couldn't force her to have a relationship with us, but we did try. Eventually, we just stopped trying, because it became clear that we meant nothing to her, then or now.

20

The Wannabes

You've heard me throw this term around quite a bit so I thought I'd clarify who the wannabes are. The wannabes won't take up too much space in my book since it's pretty simple to sum them up. They are the people who claim to be "friends of both Mark and Donny," yet support Wahlberg in his lie regarding *Entourage*. Mark publicly claimed, on more than one occasion, that Donny was "his best friend," or they were "very close friends," yet he had no problem knifing him the back. If Mark is willing to do that to his best friend, what makes these people think they have anything to gain by protecting him? My brother would never have done that to Mark if it had been the other way around. He couldn't wait to "blow up" as he would put it, just to take care of everyone he loved! The wannabes enjoy kissing Mark's ass because they really think it might get them somewhere. Hey, more power to you! They can keep on dreaming as far as I am concerned. At least my brother always stood his ground with Mark. They fought like a married couple. But I guess being Mark's "bitch" is all some people have to hold on to in life. For Donny, that just wasn't good enough.

Finally, I asked a friend of mine, who happens to work with one of the "wannabes," to get Marks address for me. I wanted to mail Thank You cards after the funeral. Mark never provided an address. So more time passed. I left the card on my sister's doorstep where my friend told me he would come by and pick it up and then pass it on to some 'middle man'. But my sister forgot to put it out on the right day when my friend came by and it never got to him. I was trying to do the right thing, but

Mark remained in hiding. I had to jump through hoops just to get a message to him! It was as if I was not worthy enough to mail a card to him directly. That's the mistake some famous people make. They think they are better than everyone else. Just remember, they sit in traffic, too.

Wahlberg used to talk to my father when Donny was alive, but then we never heard from him again. What were we supposed to think? I believe that everyone thought they could just go through life giving all the credit to Mark for *Entourage*. I hate to use the following analogy, but I want you to know how I see it.

It's like when someone is abused in a relationship or a family, and everyone knows about it, but they go on "pretending" everything is normal. They figure "nobody has said anything about it, therefore, it doesn't exist." Let this book clarify the rumors on the internet that tell the very same story I am telling you. There is a reason why Wikipedia for Turtle's character reads:

INSPIRATION

"The Turtle character was based on Mark Wahlberg's real-life assistant, thirty-nine-year-old Donnie "Donkey" Carroll. Donkey carried Wahlberg's bags for more than fourteen years while trying to launch a career as a rap musician under the name Murda One. Donkey died suddenly on December 18, 2005 of an asthma attack. Donkey and Wahlberg had a dispute earlier in 2005 because Carroll claimed Wahlberg never paid him for appropriating his life story for *Entourage*. He said all the other real-life characters had been taken care of, but that he'd been cut out."

The majority of Donny's and Mark's mutual acquaintances have made my family feel like we are in the wrong. Even people, whom I thought were very close friends of mine, are "buddy-buddy" with Walhberg. If it had been my friend's brother that was screwed over, I would stand by my friend. With the exception of the people that grew up on or around

Thornley Street, the rest of the people I knew could care less if I lived or died. And quite honestly, the feeling was mutual. Loyalty…what a joke! I hope people remember me as "Deb Carroll, the girl who didn't give a fuck." I could count my loyal friends on one hand.

These others are cowards and have no courage to tell Wahlberg that he is wrong. How can they call themselves "friends of my brother?" and then introduce themselves, as they ALWAYS do, as 'a mutual friend of Mark's and my brother's. I wonder why that always has to be established, other than guilt, hmmm?

The mind is a powerful thing. Mark really tries to convince himself that the show was his original idea because "it's about him." I don't expect to move mountains with this book, but it does excite me to know that for the rest of eternity people will Google "Mark Wahlberg" and my book will be in the list of "Mark Wahlberg" related items. Like a leech stuck to his body that he can't get rid of, the way he has been blood-sucking my family all these years. A little bit of restitution, in a way. In the same way we're stuck to this "drama" forever! I told my sister yesterday, "I can't wait to finish this book." I had to put other things in my life on hold because this is more important. And this isn't exactly the most pleasant project. Once the book is published, it means I have done all I can to get justice for my brother and I can finally live in peace. The battle will be over, the truth will be out, and that's enough victory for my family and me. Getting the truth out there was my goal. Whether people choose to believe it or not, doesn't really make a difference one way or another. The important thing is the question is out there

21

Time Heals

Ok, we all know that old saying—the only thing time does is make the horrible end of a person's life fade from your memory as you try to remember the good stuff about them. Or you can be like me, and block it out all together because the memories are too painful. According to Dr. Phil, that's the worst thing you can do. He says you should talk about things that bother you. When someone dies, it's fresh in your mind, it's raw, it's new. Suddenly, you realize you better appreciate life while you're here because tomorrow is not a guarantee.

Nothing annoys me more than when I hear people complain about petty things. I have a friend who is miserable all the time. I am not sure what went so wrong in this person's life, but this person never seems to be happy. I can't help thinking, "maybe if someone in *your* family died, you'd have an entirely different outlook." Funny thing about death, it has a ripple effect. Some people would drown in self-pity if they could. I don't think I have that right. Sure, it sucks sometimes, and maybe, there's nothing you can do to change it. We are a culture that mourns the dead. Other cultures celebrate the life of the person who dies. I have a strong spiritual awareness. I believe when people die, they are not really gone.

Luckily, my family had my sister's newborn daughter. Like God knew just when to send her, as if it were some kind of exchange. "Ok, let's take one from this family, but we'll send another one in." Is that the balance of life? My niece stole everyone's heart. We laughed at her antics and cried when we thought of Donny and how much he would have loved her. He was crazy about kids. He loved to playfully tease them and act like a little kid himself. He was just a kid at heart. He thought kids were the funniest part of life. He loved his own daughter as best as he knew how, and was always a good father.

Shortly after my brother's death, strange things occurred to our family. The first thing happened when my father went back to work. He is a believer in spirits. He was driving in his car when he heard Donny's voice, loud and clear, say, "Dad, I'm alright." He swerved a little as he spun his head around to look in the back seat to reassure himself that he wasn't crazy. It was that simple. My father has never had any unexplained things happen to him. But he knew, with out a doubt, that he heard it, even if it may have been in his subconscious mind. It was a message from Donny. If you knew my father, you could see the effect this had on him. When someone has had an experience like this, they know it happened despite the usual skepticism. Most people keep their experiences to themselves for fear of ridicule.

The incident with my mother occurred while she was sleeping. She awoke in the middle of night. She didn't see him, but she knew Donny was there. She couldn't explain how she knew, she just knew. This incident brought her some much needed peace. There is a real energy that is left behind when a person dies. You may have experienced things like this yourselves, or at least, know someone who has.

My sister and I had almost the exact same thing happen on the exact same night. It was more than a month after Donny was gone. I was back in California and I dreamed I saw my brother. Like any other dream when you can't move, run, or fight, I realized I couldn't talk. (I later learned that this is the result of the body's normal sleep paralysis, which means your muscles are asleep, but your brain is fully awake and functioning, hence dreams) So, in the dream I tried to talk, but I couldn't. From the dozens of books I've read on spirit communication, I remembered that "spirits communicate telepathically anyway," so, I figured I would try it. We were face to face, just a few feet apart, and it was just his face. In my mind I asked him, "Are you ok?" He nodded his head, yes. I asked, "Are you sure?" Once again, he nodded his head, yes. It was like being in space or something where there was no background, just dark space. His face was thin like when he was younger and much healthier.

My sister had a very similar dream in which she, too, saw him. We both told my mother about our dreams before we had a chance to discuss it with each other. About halfway through my story, my mother cuts me off, "Your sister had a dream about him, too." But it was what I said next that really grabbed her attention. "He was skinny in the dream," I said.

"What?" She asked with a strange tone in her voice.

"I said, he was skinny in the dream."

This was no surprise to me since I know that on the other side, everyone is healthy and looks that way. She told me that my sister said the exact same thing about her dream. Donny was skinny in her dream.

It all made sense to me; I did pray for him to give me a sign. I believe I got my sign. My brother was overweight at the end of his life, but when we dreamed of him, he was noticeably thin, which is why we both commented on it. These little things helped ease the pain just a little.

22

Reflections

Life went on. My sister's daughter carried us through those first hard years. It was so good to see my parents truly happy for the first time in ages. It was like Donny had given each of us a little sign. We felt we deserved to be happy. After spending a lot of time with my little niece, the urge to have one of my own really grew stronger. It broke my heart to leave her after each trip to Boston.

When she was two and a half, my sister became pregnant with her second child. I tried to get pregnant for a while, but gave up after having one failed pregnancy, and no luck after that. I just went on with my life. It's really true that you shouldn't stress over getting pregnant. As soon as I stopped caring about it, I got pregnant. The odd thing was, that both times I was pregnant, my sister was pregnant at the same time. And stranger yet, my daughter was born on the same day they were celebrating my niece's third birthday, Sunday, December 7, 2008 and the anniversary of the attack on Pearl Harbor.

I had an emergency C-section, so it certainly wasn't planned. My sister had a house full of people cheering a Patriots game (how romantic) when my daughter was born here in California. It made me feel close to home to know that people in Boston were celebrating. December is such an emotional month for my family between birthdays, wedding anniversaries, death anniversaries, Christmas…ugh! But there are times when you have to put some things out of your mind for a while and take pleasure in the simple joys of life, like diapers and baby bottles. You can't be sad all the time. Our kids deserve to have mothers who smile, even through hard times.

Having a child was truly a miracle for me. Before my daughter was born, I told my husband that I loved animals and was happy with our four dogs, one cat, twelve snakes, and three box turtles, and that if God wanted me to be a "real mother," he would give us our miracle one day. If you have kids you know that life is forever changed. Free time? Gone! But I loved it! I was on Cloud 9 and nobody was going to burst my bubble. The whole *Entourage* issue was on hold.

We talked about it from time to time, but with new babies in the family, there were much higher priorities. It was something I vowed I would do…someday. I never stopped thinking about it and always told my brother "don't worry, I'll get to it." If he were here, he'd have done it himself, and likely I still would have written about it. When he was alive, we talked about this book. He didn't like to physically write. I keep a picture of him on my dresser and I talk to it because it's really all I have. I know he hears me.

I show my daughter pictures of Donny, and she refers to him as "Uncle Donny." People joke that she is the reincarnation of him because she looks so much like him. It's just a joke, but hey…who really knows? Several people have said "it's scary how much she looks like your brother." One person used the word "eerie." But, then again, he and I look exactly alike except for our noses, and that we are different sexes. The same way everyone thought his daughter looked a lot like me. I want my daughter to know that she had an uncle who was a great man. I will tell her more about him as she grows up.

My sister had a boy this time; he is six months older than my daughter and all three of our children remain very close. Things were finally looking up in our family. My parents were overwhelmed with joy. We often talked about Donny and shook our heads when we looked at each other, as if to say "what a shame." Even when someone is gone, you can't help but think of them during moments that they would have been part of, and you find yourself saying things like, "Donny would have loved that" or "If Donny were here, he would have said…"

The whole *Entourage* issue tainted my brother's memory for us. Not only did they screw him, but we have had to hear about it for the last twelve years. It's adding insult to injury.

My brother may be gone physically, but he is a strong part of my life, especially as I am writing this book. I pray for him to help me find the right words. I tell him, "I need your help!"

We are a strong family and we all contributed to the healing process. Time really doesn't heal anything, you just get used to the way life has become. People die. It happens. Don't ever think death won't touch you at some point. Don't waste time staying mad at people you love. Imagine how your life would be if they were gone?

We were finally doing OK as a family, trying hard to remain strong. In the summer when our little ones were just babies, we rented a house on Cape Cod. It was the first time we had all gotten together. We had so much fun that we talked about this being our new "family getaway" each summer. We loved the Cape so much, and always talked about buying a house there. Then early one morning, we heard a knock at the front door. I remember my niece saying, "Someone's knocking."

Who could possibly be knocking at such an early hour? We opened the front door and, there on the doorstep, stood a whole family of turkeys. They even walked up the stairs! It was clearly a mommy, a daddy, and a baby. The daddy was, of course, the biggest of all. I had to stop my dad from making Thanksgiving jokes about the turkeys. It was such a good time, the first time we ever did anything like that as a family. It was also the last of the family vacations.

23

Lightning Strikes Twice

As fate would have it, my family was soon to face another tragedy shorty after our trip to the Cape. It was a cool October morning, I believe it was the fifth, when I noticed an urgent text message on my cell phone. October 5 was also my father's birthday. The message came from my sister and it read, "Call me right away!"

I knew my mother had gone to her doctor that morning. Not unusual, but for the last few weeks she had been complaining of pain in her stomach. My mother was, without a doubt, the "classic hypochondriac." Quite honestly, nine out of ten times she worried about ailments that didn't exist. We never worried about her, it was always my father we worried about because he had asthma like Donny. But there were two things she feared that had come true. The first one was that my brother would die before she did, and the second was that she would one day get cancer. Do our thoughts really create our realities?

My heart pounded, because just like with my brother, I knew it had to be something bad. And what could be worse than cancer? It did cross my mind simply because of my mother's grave fear of the big C. I actually thought, "Please, don't say it's cancer."

I was jumping to conclusions, after all, it was just some stomach pain. I found the courage to call my sister. It was my mother who answered. Just as before, the message had come from my sister's phone, but last time, it was my father. This time it was my mother. I had become accustomed to expecting bad news when my parents called from my sister's house. Her house was the meeting place for all my family's business.

She just came right out with it, slamming me over the head with yet another ton of bricks. Her voice was very matter of fact without the slightest hint of concern. "I have cancer," my mother said.

She further explained that her cancer was called Renal Cell Carcinoma and it was implied that this was caused by a side effect of another drug she had been taking for her Chrone's disease called, "Remicade." I admired the strength she had as she wanted to be the one to break the news to me. Usually when people have a terminal illness, they are more afraid for their families than themselves. My mother, who was usually craving the sympathy from anyone who would listen, was also slapped with reality that day.

I thought she must be in shock. I know I was! Of course, we all immediately told her not to worry. We said all the bullshit that people are "supposed to say" when someone is ill. But it wasn't just cancer, it was STAGE 4! The stages end at 4, so needless to say, it was the worst kind. As my mind raced to process the information, I told her I would be there asap. I hung up the phone and turned to look at my husband.

"She's gonna die!"

"You don't know that," he said.

"I do! I do know it," I replied.

I hated to sound pessimistic, but I just knew, the second she said it, that she would be leaving us. We were just starting to heal from the loss of Donny! We had just started planning our futures with the little ones, family trips, and all that stuff families do when grandkids come along. But fate wouldn't dare let us have our cake and eat it too. Instead, I felt lucky that my mother lived long enough to see me get married and to see all of her kids through the birth of her grandkids. But what a shame that she will not be here for them. She was the kind of grandmother who would chase the ice cream truck around the block for her grandkids. My niece (my sister's daughter) loves to remind me of that.

So, I hugged my husband goodbye, and flew to Boston with my baby daughter. I told my husband we would be there as long as we needed.

He understood. Being married to me, he had come to accept that I live in two places.

My sister had taken charge, insisting that my mother go to Dana Farber because of their extensive knowledge dealing with cancer. She went there right away and they evaluated her. We were very surprised when they told us that they thought they could actually get the grapefruit-sized tumor out, and that she would be fine. I KNEW it sounded too good to be true, but, hey, they were the experts, specializing in this kind of thing. I actually couldn't believe it, and felt way more hopeful that I had felt before.

After learning this information, I researched cases of cancer and people with stage 4 of Renal Cell Carcinoma. Everything I read said that people may live 3-5 years after surgery. I was mortified by that alone! But as a family we stayed positive and very hopeful. We reassured her that the doctors were optimistic, and therefore, we should be too.

Surgery was scheduled that same week, and I honestly think my mother was more afraid of the surgery than the cancer itself. No matter what you may believe, surgery of any kind, is always a risk. I asked friends and family to pray for her, and thought maybe, just maybe, things would really turn out alright. She was braver than even she knew she could be, and the whole family put on a brave face for her. The last thing we wanted to show her, was that we were really scared to death.

She made it through the surgery, though we honestly couldn't believe that she did. We also couldn't believe that they "got it all." Deep down, I just knew that it was a little unbelievable. I challenged the logic in my mind with what the doctors were telling me. I questioned myself a lot. I knew I had to either believe it was true, or keep the dread that I felt inside, to myself. I did believe in miracles, but I couldn't ignore the shadow of death that seemed to linger close by, robbing me of any hope I should have had.

We found out later, that during surgery she "bled out," and a team of emergency surgeons were called in. When I discussed it with the team, they told me that she lost around eight pints of blood during the surgery. None of that mattered since it appeared things were going to be just fine. Once I was back at my sister's house, I stayed up late researching more when I stumbled on some information (that I guess we should all know, but I admit I didn't) that the human body only has around 10 pints of blood! So basically she lost almost all her blood! She came that close to death! THAT was the miracle we had to keep to ourselves because she had a deep fear of blood and we didn't want to rock any boats. She was doing well; I still couldn't believe she was checking out of the hospital and going home!

The time had come for me to go back to California. She didn't want me to leave, but we joked about it and I said, "you're going to live, so I have to go back." It still felt so surreal everyday, as I thought, my mother had cancer last week, and now she doesn't. I never could wrap my head around it.

Throughout this whole process, I would talk to Donny. I would usually beg him to ask God to help us, and then follow it up with, "You better not be trying to take her from us!"

Donny and my mother had been very close. I know people will think I am crazy, but I do know a lot about spirits and 'the other side,' and I knew that if a spirit could, in fact, influence a death to get someone they want, that Donny would be the type to try.

I once read a story about a woman who had twin girls when her husband had passed away. The woman dreamed of a small white casket for months. She tried to shake the feeling of dread, but couldn't seem to let it go. One of her children did die, and she never had the dream again. She did, however, have a very vivid dream right after the death of her daughter where her husband came to her and said, "now I have one, and you have one." So, as far-fetched as even I may think it seems, I cannot deny that it did cross my mind. He was a mommy's boy! Of course, his spirit wants to be with hers. We are all connected in spirit. I recommend reading *Many Lives, Many Master's* by Dr. Brian Weiss. The book was written by a very credible doctor in Miami who was supported by his peers. This book may change your outlook on life in a very fascinating way. I am not here to talk about spirits, but I knew Donny would want my mother with him.

During this time, my beef with Mark Wahlberg was on the back burner. I would get to it, but right now, my mother was all that mattered.

As weeks passed, I got back to the routine of my life, and for a while I constantly found myself thanking God for saving my mother's life. I still couldn't believe it! My intuition is usually right, but I put any fear I had out of my mind. We never talked how about how long she had, we just cherished every second with her. When someone has a brush with death, it changes everything. Then on a Wednesday morning, the day of my fortieth birthday, I got a call from my mother. It was just thirty-four days after I had left Boston!

"It came back," she said.

I was instantly in denial and upset.

"What? They said they got it! They said we had an 85% chance!" My daughter's birthday was only three days away from mine, and I had a big party planned on Saturday morning. At this point, we thought she really didn't know the prognosis. We had assumed they could probably treat it, since whatever came back had to be small. Tumors can grow extremely fast, and suddenly we were right back where we started. The doctor told my sister that she should advise me to come back to Boston if I could. I celebrated my daughter's party wearing a fake smile, then flew to Boston the next day. There we all were, back in the hospital, at the mercy of other people who held my mother's fate in their hands.

It was decided they would try chemotherapy. But it didn't work as we had hoped. My family stood in the room with my mother when the team came to talk to us. We stared at them wide-eyed and vulnerable. All the hope we had faded when we saw the look on their faces. They were choked up as they broke the news.

"We've done all we can," one of them said.

My mother looked at them, then at us.

"We can still do treatments, right?" she asked them.

They told us that she was too weak to attempt surgery again because the cancer was draining her energy daily. The chemotherapy hadn't worked and they advised us to prepare for the worst. Trying to explain to my mother that she was going to die wasn't easy. My sister said, "Mom, you understand what they are saying, right?"

She went from being herself to being someone who could no longer talk, or eat, or anything. Ultimately, hospitals cut off any type of nutrition to people who are terminally ill. They increase the morphine dose, and the family is then treated to a horror show. For the next fourteen days, my dad, my sister, and I took turns as we watched her deteriorate right before our eyes. My heart would pound at night as I tried to sleep on the big hospital chair. All I could do was stare at my dying mother. I was terrified she would die as I watched her. We honestly didn't know if she would last a day or another week at this point. I asked the nurse, "How long will this go on?" I was referring to the sound of the labored breathing. My sister was getting ready to leave and the nurse stopped her.

"Is someone with your kids?"

She told my sister that she wouldn't recommend leaving if she could help it. I knew then that they were used to this and knew her death was imminent.

Meanwhile, all my sister's friends were taking turns watching our kids for long days and nights when her husband couldn't be there. He is a Boston firefighter and stayed home with the kids as much as he could. He didn't get to spend as much time with my mother as he wanted. But he did pull up in the fire truck one night and visited her in his dress blues when she was still coherent.

The details are too personal to get into, but we called in a priest when we knew it wouldn't go on much longer. We held hands and prayed for God to take her. She left us ten minutes later. I know God was there that day in the room because he answered our prayer. When it gets close to the end, you start praying for them to go because watching someone you love die, is the hardest thing in the world. Her official death was on December 22, 2009. It was the only day the three of us were there.

The staff commented on our family's strength and admired our love and loyalty. As hard as it is, it is important to be there for someone you love in their last moments, if you have the chance. I thank God every day that my dad, my sister, and I were there at the moment of her death.

Finally, we went back to my sisters to muster up the strength to put on a smile on Christmas day. My husband played with the kids because the rest of us were still on another planet.

Our mother was now with Donny.

24

60 Minutes

I really do try hard not to let these issues eat me alive, so instead, I attempt to use them to my advantage. It's not an easy thing to do, especially when people are on television disrespecting your family.

You may have seen the interview on *60 Minutes* a few years ago with Lara Logan "How Mark Wahlberg reinvented himself." It originally aired on July 31, 2011. (Also available on Youtube) In it they talked about Mark's career and his, then, upcoming movie, "The Fighter."

Our neighborhood priest Father Flavin, was a guest on the show and talked about how kind and generous Mark was. He was referring to Mark's many donations to the local community—said to have been "hundreds of thousands" of dollars because "he wanted to help the local kids." But could he care that his best friend's daughter was orphaned at the age of 16? What sense did it make that he would be kind and generous to complete strangers, yet not give a second thought to my niece who was bouncing between foster homes?

People from Boston who know about this, talk about it. Most recently, a mutual friend of Donny's and Mark's said, "that's really good that Mark gave Donny's daughter a million dollars." This person thought that Mark had paid my niece a million dollars. I laughed at the magnitude of that whopper!

This book is almost done, but this story is far from over. It will never be over because Mark has told so many lies that he now has to support them with more lies like this one, "that he paid my niece a million dollars." What would this 'mutual friend' stand to gain? I know him! I know he must have heard it somewhere?

I am glad I heard about this to include it in my book. I had heard a few years ago from a friend of a friend that "Mark was planning on giving my niece a settlement." I laughed when I heard it because I knew that it was bullshit. My brother died years ago! If Mark hasn't done something by now, then I seriously doubt he ever will. Who really knows? Maybe he has since paid her because he knows I am writing this book. But we know the same people. A lot of them know about this situation and ask him about it. Mark probably figures he'll never cross paths with us, so he can continue to feed his lies to anyone who will listen. The lies just go on and on! These things used to infuriate me, but now I use them to my advantage. "He paid her?" That's why she currently works three jobs just to get by! She was very offended, to say the least, about this "alleged million dollars" she had been given, and had confirmed that it was absolutely not true! I'm sure that million would really come in handy now. Even if he did give her a million dollars, she is ENTITLED to a number of the millions that was made from the hundreds of billions that came from her father's original idea! And Donny's consent form, that is filed away somewhere at HBO, is her ticket to paradise.

The interview goes on to say Mark is known as a "hometown hero" because of these donations, yet he has no problem kicking his best friend's daughter to the curb? Even if *Entourage* never existed, you would think that my brother's famous friend would have wanted to make sure she was taken care of. Any smart person would see that he does all this giving to make a good impression. Don't be fooled! As a matter of fact, his recent request to be pardoned for past criminal offenses in Boston is not because he really cares, but if he doesn't get pardoned, he will not be allowed to open a second "Wahlburgers" in Los Angeles. Wahlburger's" is a restaurant in Massachusetts that Mark is financially invested in. The rest of Marks family are very, very nice people and have nothing to do with this whole scandal.

People have come forward requesting that Mark apologize for past wrong doing, My advice to those people is "join the club!" If anyone is owed an apology, it's my family for being plagued by this drama after my brother's death. Thanks Mark!

So as the *60 Minutes* interview continued, Mark said, "If I want to be an actor, I can't worry about what anybody's going to think." But he does care what people think. He tries desperately to make up for his past by donating money in his home town. Money sure does talk.

Everyone knows that Wahlberg "cut my brother's throat." I don't know how he can live with himself. He must really not have a conscience. Luckily for him, most of the world doesn't know all his dirt that the people from Boston know. That's why I want the world to read this book, and I especially want people from Boston to read it—Dorchester specifically. I will give free copies to the people I grew up with. I am honored that anyone would read this book, and it means the world to me to have the support of the people who stood by my family throughout this whole *Entourage* scandal.

The interview goes on about Mark working on *The Perfect Storm* (in which my brother was an extra). Mark became close friends with George Clooney during the filming of this movie. It is alleged that it was Clooney who told Mark "If you want to succeed, you got to drop your friends." I may not have concrete facts about everything, but everything I write is something I have heard from mutual friends of Mark's and my brother's (some credible, some not so credible), who have no reason to make things up!

My brother wasn't the only one from the neighborhood who was part of Mark's entourage. But Mark never did drop my brother. He loved Donny; we know that. I never thought any of this was intentional, rather circumstantial; given that Mark probably had a lot of people influencing him. But we could only make excuses for him for so long. He disappointed us with his lack of respect for Donny who was more than loyal to him.

The best part of the interview was what Mark said about *Entourage*. Lara Logan talked a little bit about the show and asked him point blank, "who's idea was it?"

And Mark's answer was, "it depends on who you ask."

Lara asked him to clarify and he said, "I'd like to think it was my idea, since the show is about my life."

He'd like to think it was his idea? Of course, he'd love it if it were his idea. The simple fact that he didn't come right out and claim it, shows that he doesn't want to lie! If the show were really his idea, why on earth wouldn't he say proudly, "yes, the show was my idea." Again, he has to support the lies that are already out there.

It was clear to me that he was completely caught off guard because not only did he appear nervous, but he refuse to make eye contact with Lara. More importantly, he actually stumbles over his words! What he really said was, "I'd like to think it was my idea, since the show is about my, my, life." Does he stutter? I never knew him to stutter, but he stuttered over this question. I think they call that "a nervous stutter." He also said he has a hard time saying no, yet, he said no to my brother for ten years!

He is really egotistical to claim the show was "about his life." Seriously? My brother was part of the real entourage, and always wanted to do a show about "the entourage" because it would feature my brother as the main character who happened to work for a celebrity. Of course, Donny got the idea by working for Mark. Writers know that inspiration comes from everywhere! But to clarify—my brother wanted to do a show about "his" life! NOT Mark's life. That's why the show is called *Entourage*, and not "Markie Mark and the Funky Bunch!" The last time I checked the word 'entourage' meant: a group of people attending to, or surrounding an important person.

25

Letter To Mark

One day I was thinking about my brother and asking him to help me with this issue and in my head I heard, "the music tells the story."

I took this message to be my brother's way of telling me to listen to his music. I already knew his music, but there were a bunch of newer songs that included some comments about Mark and the show. Suddenly, it came to me, that the music really does tell the story. You can hear it for yourself at www.rezawardawgz.com.

Below is the letter I wrote Mark. Before seeking litigation.

Mark Wahlberg
9694 Oak Pass Rd
Beverly Hills CA 90210

5/27/2011
Mark,
We are attaching a letter to you written by my brother. He never had the courage to send it to you, and therefore, we are doing it on his behalf. You will see from this letter, which is plain and simple, what our issues are with you and the show *Entourage*. If I really want to get into it, I assure you, this letter would be multiple pages. On that note, we have decided to let Donny speak for himself, in his own words, in this letter he wrote to you before his death.

In short, our issues with you and this show are as follows:
This show was my brother's idea, plain and simple. No acknowledgment has ever been made to my brother for his creative part in this show. No compensation what-so-ever has ever been given, as was promised to him, by you and Eric.

You and HBO are profiting off of the portrayal of our deceased loved one which is unacceptable.

Either acknowledge my brother in some way, or cease and desist all past, present and future episodes of the show, including any movies, books, or documentary presentations relating to the show.

The truth was evident to us in the *60 Minutes* piece you did recently, which really put us over the edge. When asked, "who's idea was the show?" your response was proof to me that deep down you know the truth no matter how hard it has tried to be "hidden." In a nutshell, *60 Minutes* did their homework, which is why the question was asked to begin with.

We have to flick by *Entourage* (now in syndication) and see this show portraying our brother, who is no longer living. Do you think that is an easy thing for us, his family? It isn't, it's heartbreaking, and again, unacceptable. Just a commercial depicting "The Turtle" is tough to see. Have you ever once considered the effect this portrayal has on us?

You sent your despicable manager Eric, to my brother's funeral in your place, not to pay respect, but rather to say to my mother, "The show was not your son's idea" verbatim! Those were HIS words to my mother. As if it were a formal attempt to somehow "set the record straight."

I will personally see to it that the record is set straight. You have to know that everyone Donny associated with knows about this, including your mutual acquaintances. Many people know about this incident with Eric and my mother, and it showed us what kind of person Eric really is. For him to have said such a thing to my mother on the day she was to bury her only son, and your absence from "your best friend's" funeral, is inexcusable and my family lost all respect for you that day. It clearly shows you did not have the courage to face us.

My brother loved you "like a brother" and would have wanted us to come to you first. We will however, access other means of getting "the truth" out there about my brother, this show, and how you and HBO have exploited our family. We have tried to obtain your current mailing address through mutual acquaintances, but have been given the run around. You had someone else call me with regards to this, and even then, I asked him to have you call me. I still haven't received a return call from you or received confirmation of your address.

Do you think we don't hear this from people in Boston constantly? We do, and we are tired of it! Do I wish we could watch the show with fond memories of our brother? Of course, but we cannot. Instead, it is a "sore spot for us" and has "damaged us" and has for year's… truth be told. I wish I could be proud when people ask me about Turtle. I just wonder how you would feel if the roles were reversed?

My brother was very depressed after all that went on and ultimately that contributed in some ways to his passing. We always told him, "Mark is a great guy, he would never do you wrong." We stuck up for you so many times in the tumultuous relationship the two of you had throughout many years. In the end my brother got the short end of the stick and he was right about you. He was done wrong by you and it is not right. I know that deep down you know it.

We lost our brother and mother in a 4 year time span and as a family we are torn. We have sat on all this information long enough because we are heartbroken. Who wouldn't be under these circumstances? But, we will take whatever action is necessary so that a "wrong" is made "right" by my brother. He is no longer here to fight for what is right but we, his family are, and will by whatever means necessary to get this letter in the public eye.

Sincerely,

Debra J Carroll

P.S. Go to his site http://www.rezawardawgz.com. He raps about you in almost all of his songs. I have all the original files since I did his website. I especially recommend you listen to track #7 entitled "Close My Eyes." The music tells the story.

Of course, we never heard from Mark. However, around six weeks or so after I sent these letters to him, I received a phone call from Eric and he caught me off guard. I honestly didn't know who it was at first, so I said, "Eric who?"

And he said, "Eric, Mark's 'despicable' manager!"

Of course, some major attitude came along with that. So I did what I was advised to do by a family friend who was familiar with these kind of issues if someone other than Mark tried to call me, and told him, "You'll be hearing from my lawyer!"

Of course, I didn't really have a lawyer, but it felt kind of theatrical and good to slam the phone in his greedy ear. And yes, I still have one of those old school landlines, so he may have even felt it.

I was excited to get someone's attention, but I wasn't about to have it out with Eric because I knew I could likely say something he could use against me. I didn't want to screw anything up. I don't know a lot about the law, so I began to search for an attorney.

There have been times, I admit, that I felt bad about this. I never wanted to expose this drama about Mark because with 100% of my heart, I just knew he'd come through, but he didn't. How could he not care about Donny? Eventually, Mark may learn to live with a guilty conscience. He must be used to that by now, considering the kind of past he's had. I am not here to list everything Mark has done wrong.

I just wish people didn't put me in this situation. I am a Sagittarius and we are the "justice seekers" of the zodiac. I have often severed relationships with some friends, if they do me wrong, because I am true to myself. Some think it's OK to let others walk all over them or treat them badly. How could I ever live with myself if I didn't try to get justice for my brother? How could I not think about what Wahlberg and HBO did to my own flesh and blood? Spirits do not rest easy until justice is served. Donny deserves this recognition. He had a brilliant mind, and I think getting a credit on the show is not too much to ask. He was the creator of *Entourage,* after all, and *Entourage* was a huge success. And when this is all over, I will apply to the Walk of Fame Committee and request that Donny get the star on Hollywood Boulevard that he deserves! I know it's a long shot, but it's worth a shot!

26

Dead End Lawyers

One Boston lawyer volunteered to represent us should we decide to take it legal, however his expertise was not in entertainment law. So, of course, I looked in the Los Angeles area.

Most people might think it is cut and dry. Who wouldn't want to represent someone suing a celebrity? They could just pull the consent form and have all the proof needed that my brother signed documents! I knew this was a high-profile case and was advised to contact the famous Gloria Allred, to represent me because she is known for helping women in legal battles. She was kind enough to respond and reassured me that I did, in fact, have a case, and should act soon, but that she could not handle it herself due to her busy schedule. I was hopeful. She provided me with a referral that never got back to me. That is where the cat and mouse game began.

I ended up soliciting fourteen lawyers, and of them, three never got back to me, and the rest contacted me with a regret letter or a phone call. Nobody would put it in writing, but it was implied that the reason they shied away was because nobody wanted to fight HBO. It seemed to be common knowledge that going up against this monster was virtually impossible. I guess they never met me. I would fight the devil himself, and that's no joke.

Getting nowhere on my own, I was advised to contact the Los Angeles Bar Association because they could possibly find a lawyer who specializes in cases that specifically involve "intellectual property." Intellectual property (IP) refers to creations of the mind: inventions,

Dead End Lawyers

literary and artistic works, symbols, names, images, and designs used in commerce.

Needless to say, they never got back to me! I continued my search, feeling more like a detective than a plaintiff, since I kept receiving leads that went nowhere. It was one dead-end lawyer after the next. I vowed to never give up, but after trying fourteen lawyers and not getting anywhere, it was time to move to plan C. Some have a plan B when things don't go their way, but I had plans all the way to Z! I really did begin to get discouraged. I couldn't believe nobody would help me! I wasn't expecting anyone to care, but that noone gave a shit that I *had* proof of a real wrong doing. Typical Hollywood BS, where all the dirt is meant to stay under the rug.

Just when I was beginning to lose hope, I found Attorney Jeff in the L.A. area who was the only one who would listen to my story. He agreed I had a case. He further explained to me the reality of going up against a company like HBO, and how they would likely win because they can afford to fight, and quite frankly, I couldn't, so it all came down to money and power; the kind of things that everyday people like me don't have. However, I knew I had to get my story out somehow.

One day when Jeff and I were talking, I told him, "I think I'll write a book, because nobody can stop me from doing that." Jeff thought that was a great option because there are so many ways to get information out now with self-publishing and social media. Even in traditional publishing, books aren't marketed like they were in the early days of publishing. So I decided that writing the book really would be the best bet. You know the saying, "if you want something done right; do it yourself."

I had planned to self-publish, but it would certainly help if a publisher wanted to pick up the book.

Chasing all these dead-end lawyers could be looked upon as a complete waste of time, but since it led to writing the book, I guess it wasn't. One thing leads to another, I guess. Even as I write these words, I do not know how this book will actually hit the market, but I am sure it will!

If you're reading this, then I must have published it somehow! Wow! I never thought my first published book would be focused on a Hollywood scandal. But this book was written out of necessity. After this is over, I think I'll stop hearing my brothers nagging voice in my mind. You may think I am crazy, but I do hear his words in my mind sometimes, that I cannot write off as my own thoughts. Some, of what I hear, includes words that I don't even use. My brother never wanted to go to the newspaper, but he knew he was being screwed. Why shouldn't people know what Hollywood did to him?

As much as Donny loved Mark, he wanted the truth to come out. That's why he rapped about it, and we discussed this book shortly before he died! This book was meant to be. It's just such a shame how sad it is that my brother isn't here to really see it, and finally open the can of worms that would, once and for all, prove that he was the mastermind of *Entourage*.

I want to mention again what kind of person he was, since the focus of this book has been more situational than personal. My brother was a big teddy bear. You couldn't find anyone out there who could tell you a bad thing about the kind of person he was. He loved people and treated everyone with love and kindness. He had a nick name for everyone; a trait inherited by my late grandmother on my mother's side. He always had that little boy look on his face, and always, always had stars in his eyes. Aside from the fact that he was the sweetest and most generous person, he was also so funny. All those who knew him agreed on that.

When he died, he took that humor away from us. Nobody, with the exception of Eddie Murphy, could make me laugh like my brother could. He was just straight up comedy. Even when he was mad, I used to laugh because that little boy pout would come over his face and his forehead would get that little wrinkle between his eyes. I smile when I think of him. But what hurts more than not having him here in my life, is knowing how much he loved children, and that he is not here to be part of our children's lives or his own child's and grandchildren's lives.

27

The New York Daily News

When I was interviewed by Adam Caparell of *The New York Daily News*, I was excited, to say the least, mainly, because for once, somebody took my brother's story seriously and I knew this would help my 'then upcoming book' with a little pre-exposure. The article is as follows:

> MARK WAHLBERG ACCUSED OF STIFFING
> AUTHOR'S LATE BROTHER
> FOR INSPIRATION FOR 'ENTOURAGE' SHOW,
> CHARACTER TURTLE

Mark Wahlberg has been accused of taking the idea for his HBO show '*Entourage*' from his former friend, Donny Carroll.

Mark Wahlberg is about to be the subject of another tell-all book.

Debra Carroll tells us she's half-finished with a manuscript that will take Wahlberg to task for the empty promises he made to her late brother, Donnie (Donkey) Carroll.

She also says she'll prove that her brother—who was the inspiration for Jerry Ferrara's character Turtle in '*Entourage*'—deserves credit for coming up with the idea for the HBO show.

"For 10 years, Donny talked about 'Let's do a show about us,'" Carroll says of her brother. "And for 10 years Mark said 'nobody gives a shit about that, nobody cares.'"

Carroll says Donny was one of Wahlberg's closest friends, even before the actor became famous.

Because of that bond, she claims Wahlberg had assured her brother that he'd remember him when fame and fortune came calling.

In 2004, Wahlberg did launch a show about his dude crew, 'Entourage.' Carroll says the character of Turtle was modeled "to a T" after her brother, but that he got no credit or money.

Instead, Carroll claims, as Wahlberg's star rose, her brother increasingly felt disrespected by him. She says the two had a falling-out in June 2005.

That's when, she explains, Donny gave an interview to *The Boston Herald* complaining that Wahlberg had stiffed him and stolen his idea.

"He gave me his word that he would take care of me, and I still think he will," Donnie told the paper. "But I'm still waiting."

Six months later, Donny died from an asthma attack.

Carroll says her brother's passing was a deep blow to her family, one made worse by Wahlberg and his manager Eric Weinstein. She says Wahlberg backed out of the funeral "because he had a guilty conscience." Instead, he sent flowers and left a voice-mail for her parents expressing his condolences, but claiming he couldn't make the funeral because he "had family in town."

Weinstein, who inspired the '*Entourage*' character Eric (E) Murphy, did attend, but angered Donny's family. Carroll claimed that when Weinstein extended his sympathies to her mother, he added, "The show was not your son's idea."

She adds that her family later found a letter Donny had written but never sent to Wahlberg in which he complained that "even Eric reassured me that if I sign the consent form, I will be taken care of." When Carroll sent Wahlberg the letter in June, she says she got an angry phone call from Weinstein.

"This book isn't about putting Mark down. It's merely stating the facts of what happened," says Carroll, who vows to self-publish if she doesn't land a book deal.

And there's yet another tell-all in the works about Wahlberg, this one from one of his former bodyguards, Leonard Taylor. (See page 000)

Weinstein and a rep for Wahlberg did not respond by deadline.

Contact Gatecrasher:
Frank DiGiacomo: fdigiacomo@nydailynews.com
Carson Griffith: cgriffith@nydailynews.com
Adam Caparell: acaparell@nydailynews.com

28

Million Dollar Homes

I don't know which chapter is worse, this one or *60 Minutes*. On March 27, 2012, I was flipping through the TV channels when I came across the show *Million Dollar Homes* on HGTV.

The show started with a tour of one beautiful home and continued to feature other elaborate houses. One of the homes, in particular, seemed strangely familiar to me—as if I'd seen it before. The more I watched, the more I got the feeling that this was Mark Walhberg's house. Once I saw the basketball court and weight room, I knew it had to be because I had heard about it a hundred times. I cringed and rolled my eyes as I thought to myself 'you've got to be kidding me.' *This is Mark Wahlberg's house in Beverly Hills!*

No matter what we do, we can never escape the 'Mark Wahlberg drama.' The narrator went on to explain the different areas of the house, both inside and out. When he talked about the basketball court, I nearly fell off my chair. He said something about 'bleachers' in the court. His exact words, in reference to the bleachers, were… "and Mark says this is where he was sitting when the idea for the *Entourage* show came to him."

I was dumbfounded and couldn't believe what I was hearing. Even worse was that people believe almost everything they hear on TV! The narrator didn't know it was not true. But people are brainwashed by what they hear on the news, TV, and other media sources. Just because you hear something on the news or read it in the paper doesn't mean it's true! That's why stories are twisted and turned all the time. And who would care about all of this anyway except the family and close friends of my brother, the innocent victim?

These are the things that Walhberg allows to be said on television that he probably thinks supports his claim that the show was his idea. I am here to tell you that this robs me and my family of any peace.

The show was not Mark's original idea. Not remotely or even close! It never was, and never will be, and he and I both know it. All this drama could have been avoided IF only he had done right by my brother. Notice I made that a big "IF!" *Entourage* was Donny Carroll's original idea. Why would this even be an issue at all if there weren't some mystery surrounding it? My brother was part of the real entourage for over a decade and talked about doing a show the whole time. He had a brilliant mind and could have really been successful in the industry, if only given the chance. He learned the hard way, as many do, about the dark side of Hollywood.

Donny is no longer here to speak for himself; therefore Mark and his crooked affiliates believe it's OK to continue to spread lies and dishonor my brother by insulting him again and again. What would happen if I filled this book with lies about Mark? That would be considered slander. I believe the truth does set you free. It makes me sick that he can disrespect my dead brother, his former best friend, by implying that Donny was a liar!

It also bothers me that he just blew my family off with blatant disregard. He thinks we have no power. As far as I am concerned, he was just a kid from the same neighborhood.

I couldn't get over the 'bleachers' comment. I mean, is he kidding me? How far is he going to take this? Does he really think I am going to let him get away with this? I really don't want to have to go on television and tell the world what a dishonest person he is, but I will.

Wahlberg was not in the show, thank God. But he always seems to be in our face or he's in the Boston newspapers, as if there's nothing better to talk about.

I enjoy little victories, such as the time I pitched this book in L.A. in September (2013) and a *real* Hollywood executive expressed interest! I know my efforts will be worthwhile because I will know that I did all I could for Donny. This obviously meant a lot to me.

29

Entourage 'The Movie'

Sometimes I wonder what it would have been like if Mark had embraced our family, rather than kick us to the curb. I mean, if it had been the other way around, my brother would have done anything for Mark.

I guess now that I near the end of this, I have come to realize that I shouldn't have expected Mark to take care of Donny, especially when mutual acquaintances have told me that he doesn't even take care of his own siblings or their families. It just shows his true character. Money never buys happiness and it certainly can't buy health or family.

When I sent Mark Wahlberg the letter from my brother, it was proof in Donny's own writing, that Mark did not have permission to use the Turtle character, and furthermore, that he had been promised to be "taken care of." He wasn't looking for a handout, rather what was rightfully owed to him! Wahlberg was advised to cease-and-desist the use of Turtles character.

It surprised me that not one lawyer had the courage to go up against HBO, when the evidence is sitting in some filing cabinet out there—if it even still exisits! They just go on continuing to exploit my family's pain.

In 2013, Wahlberg was planning on making the movie *Entourage*. There had been talk of it in the past, but things had been held up because of greedy actors. (Haven't they made enough money?) Apparently, that's what fame does to people. What about the real person whom Turtle's character was modeled after? Someone else got rich portraying Donny Carroll? I'd surely love to know how things would have turned out if

Donny were still here.

Here is the full story by Lee Hernandez than ran on 10/21/2013.

Kevin Connolly on *Entourage* Movie: 'We're Gonna Do It'
By Lee Hernandez

It's been more than two years since *Entourage* aired its series finale, but fans of the HBO hit will be happy to hear that the boys will be back – this time on a much larger screen.

Kevin Connolly, who played Vincent Chase's (Adrian Grenier) manager and best friend Eric Murphy for eight seasons, told TMZ Monday that not only is an *Entourage* movie in the works, but that production on the film will begin as early as January.

"It's gonna happen," Connolly, 39, said. "It's a complicated thing, but I'm in." Connolly added that he hasn't yet signed a contract to star in the film, but assured that "everything is fine."

The actor also addressed rumors that some of his costars wanted more money to reprise their roles in an *Entourage* movie. "No, everybody's in line," he said, while teasing the movie: "It's gonna be good ... January, we're gonna do it. It's not official, but it will be."

Just last week, *Entourage*'s executive producer, Mark Wahlberg was asked about an *Entourage* movie and suggested the movie was on hold due to "greedy" actors.

"As soon as these guys stop being so greedy," the actor said with a smile, adding, "we want to make it for the fans."

Days later, the show's star Adrian Grenier seemed to respond to Wahlberg's comments on Twitter, writing: "It has and never will be about the money for me. I promise I will always stand up for the boys (that includes you) and do what I can to make sure they are treated fairly, and not be taken advantage of by anybody."

He also Tweeted some good news about the movie to a fan: "Start watching the series from season one, and by the time you finish all eight, we should be making the movie."

They talked about being treated fairly. I wonder why they would be concerned about something like that; unless maybe, they were treated unfairly before? I'm just speculating, but it sounds all too familiar to me.

Needless to say, the movie has since filmed and opened in June 2015. It is sure to be a hit; even if it sucks, people will go to the initial screening and the producers will get their money back. They know people will come. It's the same reason you see horrible sequels to good movies. Weren't eight seasons enough? The series has been nominated for 25 Prime Time Emmy Awards. And to think, my family doesn't get to be proud of something that we have a right to be proud of!

If you are a writer for TV or film, you will often hear things like "only amateurs worry about someone stealing their work" or "nobody is going to steal your idea." But this absolutely does happen. NEVER TRUST ANYONE! At the very least, register your work with the WGA!

So when the movie came out, know that my family disapproved of their perpetual portrayal of my dead brother. We contacted Mark via certified mail to get Donny's letter to him. And he got it! So he clearly didn't care, and never did. Something else that he wants to sweep under the rug.

And if greedy actors weren't enough…According to msn…

"A Hollywood acting coach who shares the same name as Adrian Grenier's *Entourage* character, has fired off a cease-and-desist notice to movie executives behind the planned film adaptation of the TV series, amid allegations that he is the inspiration for the drama.

Vincent Chase claims he met with the *Entourage* executive producer, Mark Wahlberg in the late 1990s, years before his name was reportedly used as the moniker for the TV show's lead character.

After a series of delays, the Warner Bros. film project was due to begin shooting in January, but according to TMZ, that date may now be in jeopardy after the real-life Chase issued a legal notice to prevent his name being uttered onscreen without authorization.

In the letter, Chase claims he had complained to TV bosses about his unwanted association with *Entourage* for years, and now he is finally taking action, insisting film chiefs cannot use his name without his "express permission."

Grenier starred alongside Kevin Connolly, Jeremy Piven, Jerry Ferrara and Kevin Dillon on *Entourage*, which wrapped its final season on America's HBO network in 2011.

I am not surprised that they did the same thing to someone else. That's about all there is to the story, with the exception of mystery that surround my brother's death. It's time to tell the truth about 'Turtle.'

30

Christmas

It's strange how people can become attached to things. It seems I have been writing this book forever, and have a hard time "finishing." Subliminally, it's a way for me to stay in 'Donny mode'. I can hardly believe it's taken so long and still cannot believe it has been so long since he left us.

December 18, 2017 marked the twelfth year. It's sad to know that every year my niece celebrates her birthday, will always be the same number of years that Donny's been gone. It is painful. And although I have learned to live with the losses in my life, I wonder if it ever really gets better? I have moments when I just start bawling and I wonder if it's actually getting worse. Am I STILL in denial?

My uncle Jack, God bless him, has always been a wonderful support for my family. He was a Boston police officer for over forty years which may have something to do with the way he was able to keep things real. He is my father's only sibling whom we acknowledge since the rest of his family wrote us off when we were kids. My Uncle Jack said something to me when my mother died that I don't think people usually have the courage to say. He told me straight up, "your mother is gone and you're never going to see her again." He had lost his wife years before, so he understood my grief. In the Carroll family, we don't sugar coat anything. Bostonians are straight-forward anyway; maybe too much for the average person.

I felt slammed over the head with bricks, but he was absolutely right. Thanks, Uncle Jack, for keeping it real and for being there for us in our time of need. We will never forget how you stepped up and stood beside us. But I needed to hear what he said. People are so afraid of death and the mystery of it, but it's a very real thing that needs to be dealt with! I miss my mother and Donny every day and nothing I can say could ever paint the picture quite the way I see it. It's just weird. Sometimes I think crazy thoughts like "was he ever really here?" It may sound strange, but when someone is gone from your life forever, it's just so…final.

Donny left this world on December 18. I love, love, love Christmas and NOTHING will EVER take the magic out of that day for me. However, Christmas time has become bittersweet. I will find myself singing *The Twelve Days of Christmas* with my nine-year-old daughter, and suddenly, I am overwhelmed with sadness which borders on guilt. How dare I be merry?

No matter how hard you keep your mind occupied, the workings of the mind will always find subliminal ways to remind you of important events in your life. Have you ever had a song remind you of something bad from your past? Or good, for that matter? Maybe a certain song brings on anxiety if it reminded you of a bad relationship, while another may make you laugh.

When my brother died, the world seemed to stop for the Carroll family. Yet Christmas still came and rang out it's festive and sometimes eye-opening songs like *Feed The World*. While I was standing at the funeral home dropping off my brothers clothes, everyone else was still rushing around for last minute gifts. How dare the world go on! Still, I love Christmas music!

But Christmas music is embedded in my brain as a painful reminder of my brother and my mother. I thank God every single day for my strength, and often wonder how I remain so optimistic. My motto is, and always will be, as Freddie Mercury of *Queen* sang, "the show must go on!" I sometimes begin or end that phrase with "no matter what."

When my mother was on her death bed, she still had a sense of humor. Although she joked about it, she was terrified that she would 'go' on the 18th. She was afraid of how my family would handle her dying on the same date that my brother died. I reassured her that was not likely. It was only days off and she was still coherent at this moment in time. I thought, surely, she will last a few weeks, maybe a month or more, but was I wrong. She, too, left us in Christmas week, only it was on December 22, the anniversary of Donny's funeral. Pretty morbid, huh? I spent my first wedding anniversary, December 28, 2009, at my mother's funeral. A very difficult week.

31

The Truth About Turtle

There are days when I love knowing that I am very close to getting Donny the justice he deserves, and it thrills me. But then there are times when writing down certain parts of his story are especially difficult. How do I tell the world what really happened? We can hardly wrap our heads around the truth. I have forever been telling my friends that "I am almost done with my book"! It's just hard to write this and even harder to share such a private matter with the world, but I firmly believe it is my obligation to set the record straight, besides, *the truth shall set me free.*

Donny Carroll did not die as a result of an asthma attack as reported by most media in December of 2005. Approximately thirty-five hours prior to his death, he was hospitalized for asthma-related issues. But it was not the asthma that ultimately took his life. My brother's death was a result of "acute intoxication as a result of the combined effects of cocaine and oxycodone." It was also marked "accidental." Basically, an accidental drug overdose.

It confirmed what my sister and her husband had suspected, yet not vocalized, since the moment he died. Still, it was very hard for my family to come to terms with his death as it was, let alone this further news that rocked our worlds even more. We've kept this matter private long enough. But deep down, I always knew the truth would come out. We are not ashamed that my brother died from drugs. It's not who he was, and not how people will remember him.

To reassure you that it was not suicide, since we have been asked by some people, let me remind you of the very last conversation I had with him when I practically shouted, "do you want to die?"

We had just finished talking about his health and the steps he should take to improve it; like finding a new home for his dog. He may have been depressed, but he was not suicidal. As long as I have known my brother, he was never one to take prescription drugs. He did smoke pot as far back as I can remember; it usually makes people happy! I honestly never worried about my brother being a proverbial druggie, even though drugs were all around him. He was always upbeat and happy; things were going good with Mark until the whole *Entourage* scandal.

My brother was a mommy's boy, and was terrified of dying every time he had an asthma attack. My family had been through countless 'close calls', and each time, he narrowly escaped death. His body was compromised to begin with and his lungs were weakened by asthma; the drugs just put him over the edge.

Not too long before his death, he confided to a friend that he was doing drugs. He was concerned about himself and expressed this to his friend. It was his dirty little secret, or so he thought. With the exception of a few people, it is unlikely that anyone would have known Donny was using cocaine and prescription drugs.

There were a few times, that my sister told me, when she could tell "he was on something." She's pretty credible considering she was a police officer at one time. Her husband, a Boston firefighter, suspected the same thing. We knew Donny was hurting inside over this ordeal with Mark, and who could blame him? My brother worked hard for many years and believed that Mark would not him let him down with regard to the show.

I don't know how Mark Wahlberg can go through his daily life without caring. It seems that all he cares about is money! If he didn't have a guilty conscience why wouldn't he reach out to Donny's family?

I am in no way trying to blame my brother's death on anyone. He died by his own hand. Do I believe this falling out with Mark over the whole *Entourage* ordeal sent him into a depression that led to self-destruction? I believe it did. My brother was a good person, and it breaks my heart to think of how hurt he was by someone he loved like a brother. He just could not believe Mark screwed him over. None of us could. But he did.

I think the biggest irony of all was that Jerry Ferrara's character; Turtle ends up becoming weathly in the end of the show. I thought that was pretty tasteless and an insult to my real life brother.

This is really the end of my story and I thought I would conclude with the basic message I have tried to convey throughout this book by once again; using Donny's own words.

Mark Wahlberg and Eric Weinstein along with HBO, stole Donny Carroll's original idea for a TV show about the entourage. In Donny's own words:

"I told Mark I wanted to do a reality show about me," he said. "I had an idea for a book, too. It was called *From the Hood to Hollywood, A Soldier's Story*. It was about a kid like me, who grows up with a kid like Mark, and ends up in Hollywood with him livin' the life. But Mark said, "No one cares about that."

I've been stuck on this chapter for a way too long. I need to close this chapter of my life as well, so my family can move on.

32

The Box Office

They went ahead and made the movie which debuted in 2015. There was speculation that the reason it took so long to make, was that some of the actors were demanding higher salaries. They were expecting to be paid for their creative roles in the movie, yet my brother was expected to just let his character be used for free.

It gives me great pleasure to report that the movie bombed at the box office. That, I must say, brought a long awaited smile to my face.

Thank you for reading my brother's story.

THE END

Wikipedia

In reference to Donald Joseph Carroll, I mentioned earlier that this piece from Wikipedia supports my claim. However, now I am specifically pointing out what is said about my brother's death.

The Turtle character was based on Mark Wahlberg's real-life assistant, 39-year-old Donnie "Donkey" Carroll. Donkey carried Wahlberg's bags for more than fourteen years while trying to launch a career as a rap musician under the name Murda One. *Donkey died suddenly on December 18, 2005 of an asthma attack. Donkey and Wahlberg had a dispute earlier in 2005 because Carroll claimed Wahlberg never paid him for appropriating his life story for* Entourage. *He said all the other real-life characters had been "taken care of" but that he'd been cut out.*

This information is only half right. Most media sources just assume someone checked the facts, but apparently, they did not; and just print a different version of the same story. The same way wild rumors spread that the show was Mark's idea—rumors surrounding my brother's death flew around. Nobody in my family went to the press. It was Donny's 'gold-digging' girlfriend who was hoping to make a quick buck. She took the liberty of making an announcement to the media before the official cause of death was even known. She had no right to disclose this information without first discussing it with Donny's family.

In no time the story was on dozens of websites and in the news. By the time we got the official reports, there was no going back! All the sources printed articles, yet, not one bothered to check facts! Surprised? You shouldn't be! Half of what the media says is 100% bullshit!

EndNotes

I just found out about a Leonard Taylor, a former bodyguard to the stars, who is writing a tell-all book about his experiences working for celebrities. He is especially not fond of Wahlberg, and he plans to highlight his experiences with the actor. "He filled my head with dreams then, kicked me to the curb."

Quite honestly I think it's great when others speak up. People have a right to know what goes on behind the scenes. What you see on screen is a bunch of people acting out what is usually a story based on fiction. I happen to find the real stories much more interesting and look forward to buying a copy of Leonard's book, hell, I hope to even meet him some day, perhaps shake his hand, and congratulate him for having the courage.

The difference is my brother is the one who filled Mark's big head with idea's for a show and Wahlberg took all the credit. He still tries to convince himself that the show was his idea! I know he'd like to think it was and I know he hates being asked about it because the more he lies the deeper he gets in. He's so used to acting that he forgets to be a real person. He's nothing but a weak and shallow cut-throat who profits at the expense of others.

My husband was working in LA for a music company who held elaborate parties. He met a guy there who was bragging that he was a "stand in" for Jerry Ferrara's Turtle character. My husband was dumbfounded because even he couldn't get away from it.

Links

- http://www.givememyremote.com/remote/2005/12/20/the-real-life-turtle-dead-at-39/
- eonline.com/news/795114/mark-wahlberg
- rezawardawgz.com
- http://www.nydailynews.com/entertainment/gossip/new-tell-all-book-casts-mark-wahlberg-villain-article-1.1058296
- http://www.rollingstone.com/tv/lists/the-real-life-bros-of-entourage-20150604/turtle-donnie-carroll-20150604
- http://brobible.com/entertainment/article/true-story-turtle-entourage/
- http://www.historyvshollywood.com/reelfaces/entourage/
- https://en.wikipedia.org/wiki/Turtle_(Entourage)
- http://www.bostonherald.com/inside_track/the_inside_track/2015/10/sis_tale_of_turtle_and_donkey
- http://entourageawayoflife.blogspot.com/2010/04/how-it-all-began.html
- http://ohnotheydidnt.livejournal.com/96201322.html
- https://en.wikipedia.org/wiki/Entourage_(TV_series)
- http://www.soundclick.com/bands/page_reviews.cfm?bandID=260429

Printed in Great Britain
by Amazon